101 Easy Ways
to Get Better Grades

101 Easy Ways to Get Better Grades

Key Questions Asked and Answered

by The Editors of **The World Book Encyclopedia**

Published by

World Book, Inc.
a Scott Fetzer company

Chicago

Introduction:
The key to your future

"What are you going to do?" "What are you going to be?" How many times has someone asked you these questions recently? How often have you asked yourself these questions? Often? Sometimes? Never?

If you are not concerned with such questions, perhaps you should be. You have a long life ahead of you. If this life is to be enjoyable and rewarding, you will try to fill it with not only a satisfying career but also with leisure time activities that will help you to grow physically, intellectually, and emotionally.

You have things to consider, choices to make, preparations to complete. And, compared to the rest of your life, you do not have a great deal of time to accomplish these things. The time to begin planning your future is now.

What does this have to do with whether or not you know the date of the Congress of Vienna, or the chemical formula of water, or how to spell "analysis"? A great deal, as a matter of fact. The information, attitudes, and skills that you learn today are the things that will help you to function effectively in the increasingly complex society of tomorrow.

And where will you learn many of these things? In school, of course. The time you spend in school plays a vital role in your life. How profitably you spend this time is truly a key to your future.

You are probably interested in making a success of your school career. Otherwise you would not be reading this. You may be doing well and wish to sharpen skills you already have. Or you may be doing poorly and have decided to make the commitment to "do better." In either case, the information in this book, prepared by the editors of *The World Book Encyclopedia*, is for you.

Each chapter in this book is self-contained. Each chapter concentrates upon some aspect of your career as a student or some skill that you as a student should master.

A question and answer approach has been used. Great care has been taken to make sure that the questions included are those that might be of interest to you, the student. The answers are clear and concise, each answer consisting of various suggestions that should help you to improve some area of your academic performance.

However, keep one thing in mind as you use this book. There are no "magic formulas" that will turn a poor student into an excellent student overnight. Be prepared to discipline yourself and to work hard. You are the only one who can decide what your level of achievement is going to be. And this is as it should be, because, in the long run, it will be you who will benefit as the result of a job well-done.

—William H. Nault, A.B., M.A., Ed.D.
General Chairman, Editorial Advisory
Boards, and Editorial Director,
World Book–Childcraft International, Inc.

Contents

Meet the teacher

Probably everyone knows—or at least has heard of—
a self-educated person. Through reading, observing,
listening, asking questions, and perhaps through travel,
too, such a person has acquired an education. This
person has demonstrated that formal schooling isn't
the only way to learn.

However, most people cannot educate themselves
to the point a high school or a college diploma represents. And so teachers are needed to prepare younger
generations for the future. And from a practical point
of view, your teachers give you your grades. That's
why we've started with a discussion of teachers and
how they can affect your success in school.

**1. Why might I want to know what teaching is all
about?**

The relationship between student and teacher is a vital

ingredient in academic success. Knowing something about what your teachers are doing and why they are doing it could help you to get the maximum benefit out of this student and teacher relationship.

2. Are teachers different from other people?

All professions and occupations require certain training. Members of these professions and occupations must have mastered certain basic skills. Teachers are different from any other group of people *only* because as teachers they have been trained to practice the special skills of their profession. Otherwise, teachers for the most part are approachable and responsive human beings just like you. Keeping this in mind will help you to communicate much more effectively with your teacher or teachers. And good communication is absolutely necessary.

3. What are teachers really like?

Well, for one thing, most teachers enjoy working with young people. For another, most teachers want to help their students fulfill maximum potential, not just as students, but as persons. This goal inspires most teachers to do their best.

Don't misunderstand. We're not saying that all teachers are highly competent or even dedicated. Teachers are, as all of us are, human. Like the rest of us, teachers have their hangups and shortcomings. Some are ornery or grouchy or unfair. Some are eccentric to an extreme. A few may do more harm than good.

But on the whole, teachers know and like their job. They are specialists, thoroughly trained to help students learn. And this is why you should try to learn what teachers expect from you and how they do their job.

4. What do teachers expect from students?

This is a question that is asked in one way or another by almost every student sometime during his or her school career. Yet, it is a very simple question to answer.

First of all, teachers expect students to be responsible, contributing members of the class. They prefer that students behave in a cooperative manner, displaying common courtesy toward teacher and classmates alike. Secondly, teachers expect students to come to class prepared to participate in all normal learning activities. Thirdly, teachers expect students to do assignments regularly and on time, and seek help if and when help is needed. Finally, teachers expect that students come to class equipped with whatever learning tools the class requires. These tools include any textbooks, notebooks, papers, pencils, and other items needed to do regular classwork.

5. What can I do to meet my teacher's expectations?

Approach schoolwork with the seriousness this important job deserves. If you must miss a class, make sure you have a good reason for doing it. Pay attention in class, ask questions, and make an honest effort to join in classroom discussion. Make sure that you have on hand all the tools you need to do required classwork. You can make sure you have the tools you need by using the simple technique of a check list. Many people, students and working people alike, use such a check list on a daily basis.

6. What can students expect of teachers?

For one thing, students can expect that teachers treat all students civilly and as individuals, avoiding sarcasm, belittlement, and other forms of put-down. For another, students can expect that teachers display regard for an individual student's background, interests, capabilities, and shortcomings. For yet another, students can expect that teachers know their subject well and keep up to date on it. And finally, students can expect that, within reason, teachers will be available to help when a student needs it.

7. What do teachers have to know to do their job?

Elementary teachers, most of whom teach many different subjects, must have a basic grasp of science, mathematics, English, and so on. High school teachers should be knowledgeable in at least one subject or field of study. But there's more to it than that.

Presenting material to be learned is no simple matter. Different people learn in different ways and at different speeds. A teaching technique that works for one person might not work for another. Poor presentation can kill all pupil interest in a subject.

Moreover, teachers must teach basic skills as well as content to their pupils. This task also requires the application of certain specialized techniques acquired as part of teacher training.

Take reading, for example. You know how to read. But could you teach a six-year-old how to read? Or how about a whole class of six-year-olds? What if the one method to teach reading that you tried worked for one child and not for another? Would you be capable of drawing upon perhaps a half-dozen other methods to find one that might work? Reading teachers can, and do.

The good teacher will gauge the abilities of his or her students and tailor classroom presentations to fit those abilities. The teacher will individualize instruction as much as possible.

8. How can my teacher help me?

Students, of course, turn to teachers for help with assignments, and you should do so whenever necessary. For most teachers are more than willing to listen and offer a few suggestions on how a learning problem might be solved. But many teachers establish such good relationships with students that students seek help with problems that lie outside classwork. In these cases, teachers often serve as advisors and counselors.

The role of a teacher as counselor deserves more attention than it frequently gets. Many schools have specific people called "counselors." These counselors perform a variety of valuable services. But in any school there are few counselors and many students. On a day-to-day basis teachers are more familiar with the students than counselors are.

And, while many students might doubt this, a teacher can be a friend. You probably remember at least one such teacher.

A teacher, then, is not just a person who gives assignments, tests, and marks. He or she fulfills numerous functions, all of which you should know about and take advantage of.

9. Why don't all teachers teach the same way?

Every teacher has his or her own way of doing things. A "teaching style" develops from experience, as a teacher discovers what works best for him or her, what gets the results he or she wants from students.

10. What do you mean by "teaching styles"?

Generally speaking, styles fall into two main categories. Some teachers are comfortable with a lockstep arrangement, an almost unvarying daily routine. Such teachers tend to give the same assignment to the whole class, lecture in a formal fashion, and seldom involve students in planning. They have students in the same seats each day, tend to pose questions to be answered with facts, and emphasize drill exercises.

Members of another broad category conduct classes in a less formal manner. These teachers allow students to sit wherever they please, stress student participation in planning, and emphasize class discussion and the free airing of opinion and exploration of ideas. The whole atmosphere is relaxed and individualized.

Between these teaching extremes there are numerous variations. One teacher might seem very demanding, allowing little room for error, and ordinarily assigning a great deal of homework. Another might be more lenient in these respects. One teacher might be a bugbear on assignment deadlines, another more lenient. One might inject a great deal of humor into the classroom, another might seldom crack a smile. Some teachers thrive on apparent chaos that would drive others up the wall.

Yet within all these different situations, real learning is going on. The needs of individual students vary as widely and as drastically as the styles of different teachers. An important responsibility for you, as a student, is to try to determine within which classroom situation you function most efficiently and to work to adjust if and when you end up in difficult classroom situations.

11. Is one way of teaching better than any other?

Not really. The appropriateness or inappropriateness of any teaching style is largely dependent on the kind of content being dealt with and your needs along with those of your fellow students.

Technical subjects, such as math, can usually be taught very effectively using a more formal, rigid style. However, subjects such as social studies seem to profit from the use of student participation and the exploration of ideas.

From a student point of view, much of the same is true. Some students require a disciplined approach to classwork in which all participants know exactly what is expected of them. Other students thrive in a classroom situation which permits full rein to their individual creativity.

12. But what if I just don't feel like studying, no matter what teaching style is used?

This is a problem faced by almost everyone at some point in their school career. And there is no easy solution.

One approach sometimes used by parents and teachers alike is to try to force the student to work. But experience shows that, in the long run, threats do not work very well. As a goad to learning, reward is more effective than punishment.

To be sure, lines between the effectiveness of reward and punishment sometimes seem murky. Your parents might threaten to deprive you of your allowance unless you bring home an acceptable report card. But is it the desire to avoid punishment, or the desire to gain a reward that stimulates you to work for good marks?

We're talking about *motivation*—the desire to do something. Motivation is probably the toughest problem teachers—and often students—face. You can lead a student to learning but you can't force him or her to participate. So the key is in understanding that study and learning can bring tangible rewards.

If you suffer from a lack of motivation, perhaps there is something a parent or teacher can say or do to help. Don't hide the problem until it may be too late to do anything about it. Speak up! Ask for help and direction. You may be surprised by how many people are willing to help and what can be done.

And since your parents should know you better than anyone else does, their help can become especially important. Speak to your parents about your school-work, especially if you are having problems. You may be surprised by what they can do to help.

13. What if I don't fit in with a particular teacher and his or her style?

Beware of first impressions. They can be deceptive. If you begin to have problems, try to get better acquainted with the teacher before passing judgments of any kind. Be skeptical about adverse opinions you may have heard about a teacher from other students. Students' perceptions of and experiences with any given teacher vary widely.

You should also remember that teachers are people. They are subjected to pressure, to disappointments, to unhappy experiences just like the rest of us. A teacher, like anyone else, on any given day can seem irritable, absent-minded, or not as friendly as usual. Frequently the cause lies outside the immediate class-room situation, and students should learn to ride the problem out.

14. But what if I can't get along with a certain teacher?

To get along does not necessarily mean that a student must go along. What are called personality conflicts are not always figments of the imagination or excuses for poor performance. They can be real, and you might get caught up in one. And because effective learning rests on a good student-teacher relationship, as a last resort a request for a move to another class—if such a move is possible—might be in order.

You must be sure, though, that a problem actually exists. If you feel your complaints are real and well-grounded, discuss the matter with your parents, getting down to specific behaviors that seem to cause trouble. You might find that counseling and persuasion will alter the picture, leading to the possibility of adjustment.

Counseling, of course, might draw a blank. If so, further action will be needed.

Most schools have established procedures for dealing with this kind of problem. It usually involves a conference of parent, student, teacher, and counselor or principal. Here the teacher can air his or her side, and grievances and differences can be laid out on the table and honestly discussed. Differences might be reconciled and, with adjustments, the situation given another try. If there is no meeting of the minds, then the alternative is to shift the student to another class. In the majority of cases, though, once each person understands the other's position, the situation is usually worth another try. In any event, honesty is important, as well as a sincere desire by all parties to solve the problem.

15. So, all things considered, maybe I should get to know my teachers?

By all means. And most teachers want to know their

students. The time and effort will be well spent, rewarding to all of you.

Schools commonly set aside time for regular parent visits or conferences. Students are often invited to accompany their parents to such conferences. Unfortunately, in large schools the time a teacher can talk with a student and his or her parent or parents during "open house" is limited. Sometimes five minutes must do. This is much too little time to seriously discuss any problems you might have. But at least afterward your teacher will be able to attach a personality to a name, and perhaps have some idea of who you are as a person.

If you do have problems that you wish to discuss fully with a teacher, or if you just want to get better acquainted, contact him or her and make an appointment. Teachers are only too glad to talk with students, and they will devote whatever time necessary to discussion. Teachers are normally delighted to find a student who is willing and anxious to serve as an active partner in his or her education.

How to study

Studying to a student is much the same as a job to an adult. Both, essentially, are the means to an end. Just as a job provides a payoff in terms of an income, so studying produces a payoff in terms of knowledge that will be useful for the present and the future.

True, students learn a lot without studying—in the school corridors, in the gym, in the cafeteria, and elsewhere. And some students seem able to learn enough from teachers' explanations and class discussions to get by without ever appearing to study at all. But getting by is one thing, achieving lasting knowledge another. If a student aims at the latter, he or she can't avoid the need to study.

Yet, let's face it, many students when they think of studying see themselves cooped up for hours, isolated in a closed room or a school library, faced with books out of which they must dig information. Studying turns them off. And many of the students who do sit down to study perform so inefficiently that they simply waste their time.

Like any other skill, studying is a skill that can be learned. And once the techniques are mastered you will find that the time spent does pay off.

16. Are there different kinds of studying?

Of course there are various kinds of studying. A person in an auto mechanics class might study a car's brake mechanism by watching its operation. Another in a photography class might examine a picture to evaluate its color and composition. Still another person studies the skill of throwing a basketball through a hoop by practicing in the gym.

Many students ordinarily don't come into contact with these kinds of study. Most are familiar with the kind of study involving academic subjects and books. And that is the kind of studying we're concerned with here, the kind of study with which you can most effectively make a success of your school career.

17. What if I don't think studying is important?

Obviously, the answer to the question "Why study?" is that a person is unlikely to succeed in school without study. But there is more to it than that.

At one time a person who had mastered the skills and knowledge essential to an occupation was set for life. A farmer, for example, could within a relatively short time teach his children all anyone needed to know about agriculture. Adding little, the child could pass that knowledge on in an equally short period of time.

This is no longer the case. Today, to be a successful farmer a person must know so much that it may require a college education to master the needed skills and technology. And because of the continuing "knowledge explosion" in farming as in other occupations, a college-trained farmer's children will probably need to learn even more in the future.

Rapid change has affected so many occupations that the person who does not keep up might find himself or herself washed out of a job. Newly developed office machinery forces typists to become "word-processors," a position that requires new skills and knowledge. Doctors, dentists, and engineers—among others —can scarcely keep up with new knowledge that almost daily affects their field.

Whether the task is to keep up with an occupation, or to learn a new one, the only way to survive is to study. And by the time one is finished with formal schooling, it is rather late in the day to learn how. Mastering study skills in school, and the sooner the better, is not only a means for current success. It is fast becoming a ticket to survival in the future.

There is yet another angle. Seldom, if ever, does a person have only an occupational goal in life. There are very few people today who are not involved in a hobby of some sort or who do not pursue any one of a number of part-time interests. In addition to following an occupation, you might also wish to become an accomplished golfer, or a bridge or poker player, or a member of an amateur photo or chess club. Of course, sharpening your off-the-job skills is no chore; it's pleasant activity. But even here, success at a hobby or part-time activity requires that you have the ability to study efficiently.

18. But can't I get by with cramming?

Get by, perhaps. But any more than that, no! Regardless of how quickly you learn, staying up late or all night to cram for an examination is self-defeating.

Cramming is fatiguing and irritating. Neither of these conditions leads to clear thinking, especially under exam pressures.

Moreover, while cramming might prepare a person to pass a test, after the test most of the crammed information is quickly forgotten. That which is lightly deposited doesn't stick. And since the knowledge and skills taught in many subjects build on each other, what you learn today is a foundation upon which what you will learn tomorrow must be built. This makes cramming an even more serious problem. The student who crams will never achieve total understanding of the subject. Facing the next exam, the crammer will be as helpless as before. He or she must continuously repeat the process of cramming, but with an added handicap. The further along the course work is, the more information that must be crammed.

So the best advice you can be given about cramming is "don't!"

19. Suppose I don't know the first thing about how to study efficiently. What can I do to begin?

There are many things you can do to develop an efficient way to study. To begin with, you can learn how to plan. You might call the process "budgeting time."

Every family operates on a time budget, whether a schedule is written down or not. Worktime, mealtime, bedtime, recreation time, shopping time—all fall into regular daily or weekly time slots. So should studying, and when it does, time spent studying becomes time spent productively.

20. So how can I begin to budget my time?

First, sit down and examine a typical school day. List

22

your daily activities and the specific hours allotted to each. Think carefully before you write anything down. For you are in the process of gathering valuable information. This information will be used to develop a plan for more efficient use of time. Make the list as detailed as possible. And be honest with yourself.

Begin with the time you wake up in the morning. Continue by filling in the hours until bedtime. A list of time spent during a typical school day might look something like this:

7:00 – 8:00	Woke up, had breakfast, traveled to school
8:00 – 9:00	Free time: read magazines
9:00 – 10:00	Social studies class
10:00 – 11:00	Science class
11:00 – 12:00	Math class
12:00 – 1:00	Lunch
1:00 – 2:00	Free time: talked with friends in library
2:00 – 3:00	English class
3:00 – 4:00	Gym
4:00 – 5:00	Had milkshake and talked with friends
5:00 – 6:00	Home: watched TV
6:00 – 7:00	Dinner
7:00 – 9:30	Watched TV and studied
9:30 – 10:00	Listened to records and read comic books
10:00	Went to bed

Naturally, we have exaggerated a bit to make the point. But as an example of time spent, this list hits very close to the mark for many students. Obviously, such an allotment of hours leaves little time for study. And it is very likely that any preliminary list you develop will resemble this example.

21. How should I react to an obvious problem in the way I choose to spend time?

First of all, you must recognize that a problem exists. Then you must want to solve the problem. And a serious commitment is often the best means to bring a poor situation into focus and to begin doing something about it. It is a rare student who does not want to succeed in school, and who will not, however reluctantly, eventually recognize studying as the primary means toward that goal.

Should you doubt your capacity for learning to study, or seem dubious about the connection between studying and success, try this experiment. Set up a schedule that includes ample time for study and try it for a set period of time. Then, assuming you have made an honest effort, compare results obtained using a study schedule against the results obtained before such a schedule was tried. The difference should be striking enough to convince you that the effort has been worthwhile.

22. What's the best way to go about setting up a study schedule?

First, be cautious about getting wildly enthusiastic or making commitments that cannot be met. A building goes up a brick or a board at a time. Don't convince yourself that all you need to do is to go to bed later or get up earlier, use the time for studying, and all will be well. Time for adequate rest is as important to a study schedule as any other item. Be skeptical when you promise yourself that from now on you will study during the time between the end of school and bedtime each day, with perhaps an hour off for dinner. You know way down deep that this is unlikely, and, besides, one needs more than just meal breaks from routine each day. Be sensible and realistic, willing to make progress by small steps, always on the alert for the need to adjust the schedule.

24

Remember too, if the goal is to do well in all subjects, relatively few students can devote equal study time to each. Ordinarily a person finds one or more subjects troublesome, requiring extra work to achieve success. Realistically analyze your strong and weak courses. For example, if you seem to "get" math more easily than social studies, then extra study time should be devoted to social studies.

Begin the new daily schedule with the first class of the day, allotting blocks of time according to class periods. These vary from school to school, and sometimes from subject to subject. First enter the "givens," the items already budgeted on a typical day—classes, lunch period, and so on. Then look at the empty slots. These are the primary time slots a student might use for studying. Next, decide what subjects should ordinarily be studied regularly in each time slot. For example, if there is a free period just before English class, allot that free period to preparing the English assignment for that day. A particular assignment, of course, might require more than one class period's preparation. But at least here is one block of time available for preparation.

23. Should the time after school be accounted for in a study schedule?

Most educators feel that the way in which time after school is spent is crucial to the success or failure of many students. These hours are often not completely bare of scheduled activities. You might have athletic practice, play practice for several weeks, music lessons, chores to do at home, and so on. Even so, some of the time after school *must* be allotted to study.

The first hour or so after school might be left free, as a relief valve from routine. During that time you might play ball, gossip with friends, work with a hobby activity, come home and watch television, or engage in some other relaxing activity.

This still leaves some time before dinner for practice or chores. And you might slot some of this time for studying. This, in fact, might be an appropriate time slot for "free study"; a few moments to be used if and when extra study is needed.

24. What about evening TV?

It would be unrealistic to rule out all evening television until nine o'clock or so. But "must see" and special programs by no means appear for hours on end every night of the week. So, if you find you need additional time for study in the evening, control the amount of time you devote to television. Make choices, and set priorities. After all, learning to make choices and to set priorities is an important part of growing up. And so is learning to live with your choices and sticking to your priorities.

25. How much time should be allotted to studying, in school and out?

This depends on how you are doing and, to some extent, on current academic demands. An upcoming quiz or examination might demand additional study time for a week before. Ordinarily, though, it is wise to allot a particular amount of time to a particular subject both in school and at home.

As to total study time, one rule of thumb is to plan for three to five hours of study per week for each major subject. However, keep in mind that such requirements vary from student to student and from subject to subject. Some experimentation will have to be done before you "discover" how much time you should allot to a given subject.

26. After a study schedule for a day has been completed, what then?

Organizing a study schedule for a day is just the beginning. Daily study schedules become the raw material for a broader schedule—the weekly study schedule.

An appointment book listing hours as well as days works well here. Or, you might make a weekly schedule book by ruling lines on pages of a spiral notebook, day by day, time period by time period.

The weekly schedule will show class and study time, regular after-school activities, and out-of-school study time for every day of a week. It will also list time commitments that do not happen on a daily basis, such as club meetings, athletic contests, private music or other lessons, dental and medical and other occasional appointments, and so on. The weekly evening schedule will reflect such special activities as school plays, church functions, night athletic events, and the like. The weekly schedule should also include examination dates and the dates term papers and other special assignments are due.

No schedule is immune from adjustment. Events get postponed, something unexpected comes up, finishing an assignment proves more difficult than anticipated, and the schedule has to change. Keep these possibilities in mind and always remember the need for flexibility.

Flexibility is a key element in planning. It is not the intent of planning—budgeting time—to encase you in a straitjacket. Rather, the goal of planning is to help you take into consideration the various demands school and other activities make, and to balance these against your own needs. A realistic schedule provides time for study, and also allows ample time for relaxation, recreation, the pursuit of hobbies and other special interests, and for just "fooling around." Remember that time is precious, not something to be wasted. A well-thought-out approach to the use of time, together with the willingness to set and accept priorities, will pay you great dividends in the amount of time made available for any activity.

27. What if I have a part-time job?

A part-time job naturally takes away from the time available for other things, including study. As one more "given" on a study schedule, a part-time job forces a close examination of priorities and goals.

This can be a difficult problem. Work experience is valuable to a person in junior or senior high school. It serves as an introduction to a world he or she will be a part of for much of a lifetime. Work experience can help build a person's sense of responsibility. Investigations have suggested that many students with part-time jobs *and* a sensible study schedule make better use of their time than those with neither. Students who have many things to do tend to be much more serious as to how they plan to spend their time.

On the other hand, a job can serve as an excuse for not studying. It can, whether used as an excuse or not, be a cause of poor performance in school. And even though a person may keep up well with both work and school, a job often cuts severely into the time available for recreation and rest.

Here, as in many other situations, it's the specifics and not the generalities that count. Whether you can manage both school and a part-time job depends on you. This is a situation you must watch over carefully. And it is a situation that will especially benefit from the use of a well-thought-out study schedule.

28. What about studying on weekends?

This also is an individual problem requiring individual-ized solutions. Some students can budget and make such efficient use of time during the school week that weekends can remain entirely free for recreation and relaxation. Other students can't do so well.

Most students reserve Friday and often Saturday night as well for school activities, dates, and other social affairs. Most families set Saturday aside for miscellaneous chores and shopping, and some fami-lies provide time for watching a televised athletic event in the afternoon. Many students schedule week-end study on Sunday afternoon or Sunday evening when thoughts usually turn to another week of school. For a good many students, this is sufficient. But, again, much depends on the individual. In making up a weekly schedule, though, a student should decide about weekends and stay with the choice.

29. Where should I study?

You probably have assured your parents that you can study and watch television at the same time. You probably have told your parents that music playing in the background or having your friends around you help your concentration. But don't believe it.

Certainly one can learn to divide attention, and surely a person can learn *something* studying in front of a television set, or with music in the background. But not much. Any distracting element cuts efficiency. Having a television set or radio on, lying sprawled on the floor or on a sofa, munching a snack, gazing out of the window—all distract from effective studying.

Studying is a personal and lonely task. And it de-mands active, concentrated participation. It should take place in a quiet atmosphere, free from normal traffic patterns, and in the same spot each time. The work surface should be permanent, a table or a desk, and the chair upright but comfortable. All tools for study—books, dictionary, paper, pencils, and so on—should be within easy reach. The student should face a blank wall while studying, again to eliminate distractions. Lighting should be adequate and nonglaring. Ventilation should also be ample, and the temperature kept at around 70°F. (about 21°C).

The ideal study room is one used for that purpose alone. The next best room is the student's bedroom.

For any one of a number of reasons, few students are able to study in an ideal atmosphere. You might have to share a bedroom with a brother or sister. Space may be so limited that the kitchen or dining room table must do. But such obstacles are not insurmountable. Brothers and sisters can study in the same room if necessary. Other people can keep out of the kitchen or dining room during study hours. The main point is that studying should be regular, concentrated, in the same place each time, and in a quiet atmosphere.

30. What is a student's main study tool?

The textbook, a book designed especially for study, is your main study tool for most subjects. Authors write textbooks according to a detailed outline, and important points frequently become chapter subheadings. These and important words and ideas often appear in **boldface** or *italic* type. In addition, textbooks contain illustrations, maps, and charts and graphs to aid learning, and usually include questions at the end of each section to help students review material more effectively. In some textbooks, questions or an outline also precede each major section.

It might be helpful for you to identify such features in your textbooks. Familiarize yourself with these books and pick out the various built-in aids to learning all such books contain. Then check to see if you use them. You might be surprised to find out that, like most students, you don't take advantage of such features. And you may not even be aware of their significance.

31. Is there any specific method for study I can use?

The SQ3R method of study is one specific method that has proved valuable to many students. "SQ3R" stands for the terms *survey, question, read, recite,* and *review.* This method works especially well when applied to the study of textbooks.

To *survey* a textbook means to read the subheadings, activities, outlines, and any study aids given in the chapter or section being studied. These may be few or many. But they represent the framework around which a textbook is built. These features introduce the material to be learned.

For example, in a chapter dealing with the ancient world these subheadings might appear: "The Greeks before the Persian Wars"; "Persia and the Greeks, to 478 B.C."; and "The Athenian Empire, 478–404 B.C." These signal you what the general direction of the information in the chapter is.

The next step is to turn the subheadings into *questions.* Such questions might be: "What happened in Greece before the Persian Wars?"; "What were Greek-Persian relations up to 478 B.C.?"; and "How might one describe the Athenian Empire?" These questions serve as a broad guide to study. The questions will usually tip you off to what the writer of the textbook considers to be the important information. You should make a written list of all such questions.

Now let's look at the textbook more closely. Under each of the subheadings, minor headings appear. For example:

The Greeks before the Persian Wars
   What the Greeks Were Like
   Revival after the Dark Age
   The Polis: Sparta
   Colonization
   And so on.

You should turn these headings into questions, too: "What were the Greeks like?"; "What was the Dark Age and the revival afterward?"; "What characterized the polis of Sparta?"; "What part did colonization play in Greek history?" At this point, you should identify any unfamiliar words. All these words should be looked up.

And now, with a framework of questions in mind, you should begin to *read*. While reading the material carefully, you should study any pictures, charts, graphs, maps, and other visual aids. Usually, any information worth a piece of illustrative material is important. The next step is *recitation*. This means answering the questions you constructed earlier, using information you are able to find in the book. As an aid to recitation, while reading you should underline key or unfamiliar words or phrases, write them down, and also record key ideas.

You can look unfamiliar words up in a dictionary as you go along. Or, if skipping an unfamiliar word temporarily does not block your understanding greatly, you might note such a word and find its meaning later. Some meanings leap out from context. For example, a reader might catch the meaning of a word such as "divinity" from a previous phrase "all-powerful single god." In any case, at some point you should master the meaning of all the words in an assignment in order to fully understand the assignment.

The final step in this method for study is *review*. Preparation for this final step should begin during the stage of recitation. While studying the assignment, you should construct an outline, using the most important idea you are able to find in each paragraph. The basic framework for such an outline should be the list of questions you constructed earlier. Such an outline might look something like this:

I. What were the Greeks like?
   A. curious about everything
      1. wanted to know about everyday things
      2. also wanted to know about such deeper questions as what universe is like and what causes disease
      3. did not insist on final answers
   B. religion
      1. had many gods
      2. believed gods had some influence, but believed more in the power of human reason to solve problems

The review procedure should include study of the outline, restudy of all headings and subheadings, and rereading of key portions of the text. Finally, you should complete any activities and answer any chapter and/or section end questions contained in the book.

All of this written material should be kept, carefully filed. The material will be vital later when you must prepare for tests.

The SQ3R method might seem like a slow and laborious way to wring meaning from an assignment. It is. But it is also a tried and true path to understanding what you read. And, as with so many other things, the more you use the method, the easier it becomes. Questions gradually become easier to formulate. You begin to recognize key points and ideas more quickly. Reading becomes more concentrated and information is absorbed more easily.

However, if you do decide to try this method, remember that you must be patient. Results over the

short range will be meager. But if an honest effort
is made in the application of the SQ3R method, the
long-range payoff will be substantial.

32. How can I get the most out of classroom time?

A teacher frequently emphasizes key points during
class. A teacher will often tag an item as important by
calling it so, or by saying "Remember this," or "I emphasize this." Whenever you hear such phrases, write
down the information that follows. This information
should then be reviewed later while studying.

Class lectures become important in high school, and
even more so in college. In lecture classes, listening
and note-taking skills become vital. Concentrate ex-
clusively on what a teacher is saying in a lecture. A
good lecturer will signal major points with voice
changes, by providing examples, by leading in with
such phrases as "here are three reasons," and by an-
nouncing a summary.

Do not try to write down every word the teacher
says. It is best to take notes in outline form. Such an
outline is probably the most effective tool for review
you can have.

Should you know shorthand, so much the better.
Few students do, but anyone can make up a personal
shorthand, useful for taking notes. One has only to
learn to abbreviate. Use "div." for "division," "corp."
for "corporation," "dev." for "development," and so
on. Drop such unnecessary words as "a," "an," and
"the," and such word endings as "-tion," "-ing," and
"-ment."

You can check your listening and note-taking skills.
Ask someone to read to you from a textbook while
you take notes. Then go over the notes together to
see that the important points have been included.
Keep practicing until you are satisfied that you have

developed an acceptable level of listening and note-taking skills.

Finally, participate in class discussions, especially by asking questions. You can gain additional information as well as clear up foggy points by asking questions.

Tips for better reading

Students learn from television and from radio. They learn from lectures, from listening to tapes and records, from pictures in books and magazines, and from class discussions. They learn during the normal give and take of conversation. But mostly students learn from reading, the backbone of any formal education.

As television developed right after World War II, some observers foresaw a time when reading would be obsolete. A few people might still have occasion to read, but the majority would learn from television. Television would become the primary educational device.

We know now that this prediction was in error. There has been no decline of the need—or the desire on the part of many—to read. Success in school courses still depends, to a greater or lesser extent, on an ability to read. And those students who cannot read, or at least cannot read well enough to master material, are in trouble.

The only class in school that might possibly not require reading is physical education, although students often face written examinations here, too. And written examinations must be read before they can be responded to. There is reading in home economics —directions and recipes, if nothing else—in shop and auto mechanics classes, in the science lab, and certainly in such courses as social studies and English. There is no way around the fact that most academic courses rely heavily on textbooks.

No one knows precisely how a person learns to read. Many methods of teaching the skill exist, each of them effective to some extent, none of them surefire for every student.

The majority of students learn to read at least well enough to function. Yet even though every student is exposed to reading instruction at least from grades one through six, a distressingly large number fail to master the skill. And just as the individual process of acquiring an ability to read remains mysterious, so too in many cases do the reasons why many students fail.

If you have a reading problem, by all means take advantage of any help your school has to offer. If you are a good reader, which means primarily that you are able to comprehend the material read, you have little to worry about. On the other hand, if you are a mediocre reader—which probably describes the majority—able to "get along" but little more, there is room for improvement, and you can help yourself.

33. How can I know if I have a reading problem?

One signal, of course, is poor marks, especially in classes that require heavy reading. It appears that the student isn't getting much from textbooks.

Reluctance to read for any purpose is another sign. Most people who read well read a lot because it gives them pleasure.

Still another is complaints about having to read so much. These may appear even when reading assignments are relatively light.

Investigation here might reveal problems calling for expert help from a reading specialist at school. On the other hand, the difficulties might be the kind that you can begin to solve for yourself.

34. Is slow reading a problem?

Many students have trouble because they read too slowly. This applies even to some who comprehend fairly well. And it's a handicap, especially when reading requirements become great. It's not uncommon for a teacher to hold students responsible for the contents of one or more chapters of a thick textbook each week. Because most students have other reading assignments besides, the slow reader soon falls hopelessly behind.

35. Why do some students read so slowly?

Subvocalization, for one reason. What does that mean? Consciously or unconsciously a student may go through the motions of reading orally without making any sound. In some cases, he or she moves the lips. In others, he or she may mouth words without lip movement. In either case, the student can read no faster than he or she normally speaks, at best a few more than a hundred words a minute. It's a terribly inefficient way to read.

Another cause of reading slowly is concentrating on each word individually, even if one doesn't subvocalize. This is not an effective means of reading.

Running a finger along line by line under what one

reads is another factor that slows reading speed.
This makes reading almost painfully slow.

Lack of adequate vocabulary also slows a reader
down. A student with only a meager command of
words tends to stumble over each word he or she
doesn't know. The more conscientious students use
a dictionary. But even so, the need to consult a dictionary frequently during every reading assignment
consumes time.

Finally, the tendency to reread helps slow a reader.
After reading a sentence or two, a student with this
habit goes back because he or she failed to get the
meaning the first time around. This naturally reduces
reading speed.

36. How can I break poor reading habits?

You can check on whether you subvocalize by observing yourself while you read. Don't be satisfied just
because your lips aren't moving. Place your fingers
against your throat. Even if the lips are tightly sealed,
movement of the vocal chords will betray the sub-
vocalizing habit.

And this habit will not disappear unless you apply
real effort. It's a matter of self-training and self-
discipline. A significant increase in reading speed will
usually solve the problem of subvocalization. Tips to
increase reading speed will be given later in this
chapter.

As to the finger tracing habit, raising the reading
rate will usually eliminate this problem, too. But
in the beginning, if necessary, hold a pen, pencil, or
ruler in your hands as you read.

Learning to read faster will also help solve the word-
by-word syndrome and the habit of rereading. As to
vocabulary problems, a later chapter in this book is
devoted to techniques for building a more effective
vocabulary.

37. What is the most serious reading problem?

Lack of comprehension. Failure to understand the material makes reading a waste of time for many students. Lack of comprehension is one of the more serious reading problems because it is probably the most difficult reading problem to deal with.

38. What causes lack of comprehension?

Subvocalization, word-by-word progression, rereading, lack of vocabulary—the same items connected with reading at a tortoise-rate—all help to limit comprehension. Another cause is failure to concentrate. Daydreaming and reading comprehension don't go together. Neither do reading and background noise, such as radio or television.

39. Which is more important, reading speed or reading comprehension?

If you have to choose, you should take comprehension over speed. But actually, at least up to a certain point, these two reading skills do go together. The point of diminishing returns sets in when the eyes move so fast that the brain is receiving only partial messages, fragments that the brain is unable to fully comprehend. But most readers have a long way to go before reaching that point.

As a student learns to read phrases instead of words, increases the vocabulary, masters the art of really reading silently, and stops rereading, speed increases. The discipline required to make these skills work forces the reader to concentrate. And concentration improves comprehension.

Remember, though, speed and the difficulty of

material are related. A student must spend more time on a highly technical passage than on an ordinary novel. For maximum comprehension, the rate of speed must be adjusted to the material.

40. How can I increase my reading speed?

First discover what you're building from. Find out your reading speed. You can easily test it.

Select a piece of expository material—a passage that explains or reports on something—that is not highly technical and totals about 300 words. This might come from a magazine, a newspaper, a book, or an encyclopedia.

You can test comprehension at the same time as you test speed. Simply develop some questions to ask yourself about the content of the passage. Identify content that lends itself to the following type of questions:

a. a question that requires the reader to identify the main idea in the passage
b. a question that asks for a fact or a detail
c. a question that calls for the definition of a word or term
d. a question that requires the making of a judgment or an evaluation.

Use of the three exercises below will give you a more complete idea of where you stand in reading skills. Each exercise is about the same general topic. Each is about 300 words long. Each is followed by four questions. And each exercise has been written at a different level of reading difficulty. The first exercise is written at an upper elementary school level. The second exercise is at about the junior high level. The third exercise is at a high school reading level.

History of Television (first level)

Almost everybody watches TV today. This may seem funny to people who are the same age as your parents or grandparents. That's because TV didn't even start until after they were born or grown up.

Now almost every house has a TV set in it. One-third of all families have two TV sets. Some people have more than two TV's. More and more people have color sets every day.

All of this started in the 1920's with experiments. They were tried out with all sorts of different machines. Finally one company decided to put TV's in 150 houses around New York City. They made up programs just for those people. The first one was a cartoon of Felix the Cat. This started in 1936.

The companies had to stop doing these programs after five years. That's because the United States started fighting World War II. The TV companies had to work on other machines that were used in the war instead of just for fun.

Once the war was over, though, TV came back. At first, you could only watch TV if you lived on the East Coast of America. Soon the programs were sent all over the country.

In the 1950's, people got interested in a big way. They would stand on sidewalks to watch TV's in store windows. They would go over to friends' houses to see a show. Sometimes the first family to get a TV was sorry. Their house would be full of friends all day long. They would hardly get to watch the set themselves.

The first color shows were tried in 1953. Almost nobody had a color set. After 10 years, lots of people had bought them even though they cost a lot more. Almost all shows are now in color.

(Note: This selection is written at an upper elementary school readability level.)

1. Where did people go to watch TV when it first became popular?
2. Why did companies have to stop sending TV shows in 1941?
3. What does the word *programs* mean in this story?
4. How would you describe the way Americans got interested in TV in the 1950's?

Programs on Television (second level)

Programming on television has changed a lot over the years.

The first shows were mostly entertainment. Cartoons, comedy, and variety shows took most of the time. Quiz shows were very popular. They were a little different from the game shows of today because big money went for straight questions and answers. There was a big scandal, though, when people heard that the answers to very hard questions had been given to the winners before the shows.

Public affairs and news programs started early in TV history. The groundwork for this was laid when the first coast-to-coast broadcast showed President Harry Truman beginning the peace treaty meetings with Japan in 1951. The U. S. Senate allowed TV cameras to film its investigations, too. The public was able to see one committee question mobsters about crime and the Mafia. Later, they could see very emotional meetings when one senator, Joe McCarthy, accused thousands of people of being Communists. This kind of coverage was continued in the famous Watergate hearings that investigated President Nixon and his staff.

One thing that many critics point out is that TV has brought a lot of violence into homes. They say that early morning cartoons and nighttime dramas show too many fights and killings. It is true that TV news programs have shown more real-life violence than ever before. For example, millions of Americans saw Jack Ruby shoot the man accused of killing President Kennedy. Millions also saw the war in Vietnam on TV every day. Some people think this should be controlled, but others do not.

One kind of show that has remained popular and almost unchanged since the beginning is the soap opera. Once soap companies did sponsor them to reach housewives during the day. Now they are popular with many different audiences and have a wide range of sponsors.

(Note: This selection is written at a junior high readability level.)

1. What is one thing critics say TV should not have brought to American homes?
2. Why was there a scandal about the early quiz shows?
3. What does the term *public affairs* mean?
4. How has programming on television changed over the years?

Light Splitting in Color TV Cameras (third level)

The color TV camera performs a whole range of complex tasks so that the image before it will reappear before your eyes on a TV set. Most TV transmissions now are in what is termed *compatible color*. This means that the signals may be received on a color set and result in a color image or they may be translated into a black and white image if the receiver is not a color producer.

The spectrum of color is produced by mixing the three primary colors just as an artist does. Yellow and blue mixed result in green, and so forth.

The job of a TV camera begins when its lens captures light from the scene in front of it. It must split this into three images, one for each primary color. *Dichronic,* or two-color, mirrors are used for this process as blue light is bounced from the first mirror, allowing red and green to continue. Then the red elements are reflected and green is allowed to pass through. The three separate light beams are then processed independently by the camera until your eye reassembles them on the TV screen.

A pattern of electric charges is created by the light striking a target area. As electrons flow from the area, they become the signal to your TV set to show that color in a glowing dot in a tiny area.

Because the signals are separated by color, TV cameras can be made to block out anything that's just one color. This device is used to insert weather maps or scenes from other places. One area in the main scene is painted all blue, for example, then at the desired time all the blue light signals are blocked. A second camera can then fill in the "hole" with the desired picture.

(Note: This selection is written at a high school readability level.)

1. What is the primary function of the TV camera?
2. Why can TV cameras be made to block out anything that's just one color?
3. What does the term *compatible color* mean?
4. In what form is light transmitted from the TV camera?

Now, using a stopwatch or a watch or clock with a second hand, time yourself as you read the appropriate passage. Then find the rate in words per minute, using the following formula:

$$\frac{\text{number of words read}}{\text{time in seconds}} \times 60 = \text{WPM (words per minute)}$$

If you read the entire passage in exactly 60 seconds, your WPM rate would be 300 (300 divided by 60 times the 60 seconds in a minute). If the task required 120 seconds, the speed would be half that, 150 words per minute.

Once you have determined your WPM rate, test your reading comprehension. To test this, answer the four questions that follow the passage you read. Remember, no reference should be made back to the reading while the questions are being answered.

If you correctly answer all four questions, your comprehension is good. If you miss one, that is still acceptable. Two or more wrong, though, generally indicates a problem of reading comprehension.

Perhaps you didn't understand some key words, or perhaps you pushed speed at the expense of comprehension. At first there is a tendency to do this, owing probably to a natural inclination to want to score well. But as was mentioned earlier, speed and comprehension are inseparable twins; they must be brought along together.

For most students, a reading rate of 200 to 300 words per minute is normal. A person might fall to half that if the content is technical or difficult for some other reason. On the other end of the scale, a person might go up to 350 to 600 words per minute when reading a newspaper or a magazine and up to a thousand words per minute if he or she is skimming a novel. When reading a school assignment, a student must allot time according to the type of material to be read.

To be of real help, you should check your reading speed frequently, using a variety of different material. And you should practice regularly to try to raise the rate. It's a strain, at first, but with the passage of time it becomes easier, even a matter of habit.

41. What else can I do to improve reading speed and comprehension?

Two to three hundred words per minute is not especially fast. The average reader can improve upon that by following a few suggestions.

One is to avoid concentrating on single words. For example, consider this passage.

"Being   able   to   get   a   tan
and   build   muscles   is   part   of
why   city   lifeguards   want   their
underpaid   jobs."

Hard to read? Sure. Moving from word to word tires the eyes, yet many people read this way. By the time the reader reaches the end of a sentence, the opening words have been forgotten.

What's the alternative? Reading in phrases. Let's divide the words in a different way.

"Being able   to get a tan   and build
muscles   is part of why   city lifeguards
want   their underpaid jobs."

This is easier to read, and one can absorb it more quickly. The eyes make fewer stops when reading phrases than they do when reading individual words.

A person's visual span, or peripheral vision, is the key here. Almost everyone has it. But many don't use it while reading, and even fewer try to stretch it, which is possible with a little effort. If you fix your eye on this ° you can see and take in several words on both sides. Set up some practice exercise to improve your visual span. All you need is a ruler, a pen, and a newspaper. For example:

> Did you know that you are doing things all the time because of tiny changes in your body? Nerves send messages from little bits of information that can affect what you do.

Fix your eyes on the line and move them steadily down it, trying to see as much as possible to the left and right of the line. Keep practicing until utilizing the visual span becomes a habit. You will, or should, quickly see how this can be transferred to reading textbooks, many of which have double-columned pages. Eventually you will be reading wider columns, phrase by phrase. And this will help increase both the reading rate and comprehension.

To keep track of progress, chart the results of the reading exercises you do. The chart will probably show a ragged line at first, the rate rising and falling. The general trend, however, should be upward. Then at some point the rate will become stuck on a "plateau," changing little over a series of exercises. This is a normal pattern in the development of any skill, so don't become discouraged.

At some point, comprehension and speed will part company. That will mark your maximum rate, at that particular time. But now you should be able to leave the problem with the assurance that both reading rate and comprehension are higher than they were in the beginning.

42. Should I learn to skim or scan reading material?

Yes, these are both techniques you should master. Both skills are useful and they can be learned easily with practice.

Skimming involves moving quickly over a page, looking only for highlights, key phrases, headings, and the like. Skimming is especially useful for review, and as an introduction to the main points of a chapter in a textbook. Underlining key words and phrases and topic sentences aids skimming.

Scanning involves an equally high rate of eye-movement. Here, however, the reader is concerned with finding only a few items.

A reader uses the skill of scanning when he or she looks for a name in the phone book. There is an image of a name in the mind, and the reader ignores all other data on a page while quickly searching for a name there to match the image. A reader scans when examining an index, searching for a particular entry. A reader uses the skill of scanning when doing research, going through numerous books to see if they contain useful information, ignoring all the rest.

Skimming and scanning are not reading as the word is usually understood. But they involve reading, and are especially useful skills when a reader is looking for pieces of specific information or for review. The average reader can pick up these skills quickly.

43. How can I get the most out of reading a textbook?

Most reading in relation to school matters involves textbooks. There are various ways to approach the reading of a textbook that will help improve comprehension.

Before you tackle a textbook, look it over, or survey it. This is something you can do easily.

First, examine the table of contents, unit and chapter titles, and any subheadings that might appear.

These elements will give you an overview of the book.

Then examine the book's back matter—a glossary of terms, perhaps a list of additional readings, and the index. The index is there to help you locate needed information quickly. The more thorough the index the better. The other aids can help you during review time as well as serving as a source of quick information.

A book's preface and/or introduction will tell you more about the book and its purpose. Then as you flip through a textbook, you will note chapter headings and subheadings, perhaps some material in italic or boldface type. Each chapter will probably have an introduction, outlining the contents, and perhaps a summary paragraph or two at the end.

Note the textbook's graphs, charts, illustrations, and maps. Sometimes these supplement the reading. In other instances, they convey additional information.

Finally, most textbooks contain questions at the end of sections, chapters, and units. These are valuable guides to improving your comprehension.

44. Is it important to read with a purpose in mind?

Yes. You must establish a purpose for reading. Knowing where you want to go increases your chances of getting there.

You might read for a general impression of the main ideas and a few details. Reviewing for a test, you might go a little more slowly, looking closely at particular details and ideas, asking questions, mentally fitting pieces of information together. The SQ3R method could be profitably used at this point.

If reading fiction, you might concentrate on how the author handles character, comparing one person in the book to another. Perhaps the purpose might be to see how an author handles description. You will then read with that purpose in mind.

It matters little what the purpose for doing the reading is. Obviously, this purpose will vary from reading to reading. But it is important that there be some purpose. This purpose gives you as the reader a fixed point around which information may be organized.

45. How important is it to identify the topic sentence of a paragraph?

Locating and noting topic sentences are an excellent way to aid comprehension.

A good paragraph makes one and only one point. And somewhere within that paragraph, as a rule, there is a topic sentence. In many cases it is the first sentence in the paragraph, but the reader should not depend on that. The topic sentence might appear at a paragraph's end. And we inserted the caution "as a rule" above, because some writers, and good ones too, sometimes don't include an obvious topic sentence. The paragraph will still contain only one point, but the writer leaves it up to the reader to discover what that point is. This is not a trick; it is simply a matter of writing style.

Let's look at some paragraphs.

The spread of American food crops was the other great change that transformed the African scene in these centuries Maize and sweet potatoes became the staples of west African agriculture, and maize spread throughout the continent. The additional food supply thus made available may have permitted population growth so rapid as to make up for the losses to the slave trade. Although millions of innocent captives were sent to the New World to labor in the plantations of Brazil, the Caribbean, and the southern colonies on the North American mainland, there is no sign of lasting depopulation of African territories. (William H. McNeill, *The Ecumene, Story of Humanity*. Harper & Row, 1973, p. 505).

Where is the topic sentence here, the one that tells what the paragraph is about? It's the first sentence, of course.

William was a vigorous king, but he was mainly interested in his wars against Louis XIV on the continent. As long as his new kingdom supported such wars, he was well content to leave the government in the hands of ministers agreeable to Parliament. Queen Anne (reigned 1702–1714), George I of Hanover (reigned 1714–1727), and George II (reigned 1727–1760) followed the same policy. They found it simpler to govern when their ministers could get support for their acts in Parliament. Indeed, both the kings, George I and II, did not speak English easily and stayed away from most of the meetings of the ministers at which government policy was discussed. They were satisfied, as a matter of fact, to give the responsibility of choosing ministers to Robert Walpole, an ordinary member of Parliament who was able to win the confidence of both the monarch and of a majority in Parliament. In common speech he came to be called prime minister; and the group of ministers he selected were referred to as the cabinet. (*Ibid.*, p. 475.)

Where's that important sentence here? The first? No! The paragraph tells you nothing about William's vigor or his wars with France. It's simply a transitional sentence. The heart of the matter lies in the second sentence, although you must be careful here. The key lies in the phrase "well content to leave the government in the hands of ministers agreeable to Parliament." The author uses William as a lead into his main point, an example of how Parliamentary power grew in England. Let's look at another paragraph.

> Britain's internal political development was almost exactly opposite to the French experience. When the Stuart kings first came to the throne in 1603, they tried to build an efficient royal government like the French. This soon got them into trouble with Parliament, a medieval institution that got in the way of efficient administration by refusing to grant needed taxes and by defending unruly groups that refused to obey the king in matters of religion and taxation. Indeed in 1642, relations between Charles I and Parliament got so bad that civil war broke out. Parliament won, and in 1649 a special commission decided that King Charles should be executed for failing to keep his promises to Parliament. But cutting off Charles's head solved nothing and, in fact, shocked many Englishmen.
> (*Ibid.*, pp. 474–475.)

Which sentence here tells the reader what the paragraph is about? Not the first, nor the second. But do you see why it's the third? The paragraph is mainly about Charles I's relations with Parliament.

Now for a paragraph that has the topic sentence in yet another place:

> When I awoke I didn't dress immediately, attending first to breakfast and correspondence for a couple of hours. Then I dressed and went out, strolling for

an hour or so along the river bank. Recalling that my food supply had run low, after lunch I visited my favorite shop to arrange for restocking. I then lounged for a time in the coffee shop, returning home pleasantly tired and in good spirits late in the afternoon. This is how I spent that day.

Where is the topic sentence? At the end of course.

Topic sentences are hooks upon which to fasten the threads of a paragraph that form a fabric of meaning. A person can train him or herself to spot them. Once they're found, comprehension increases because a person has a point around which to cluster the other sentences and hence organize the meaning of a paragraph.

As a starter, hunt for topic sentences and write them down. Then read the paragraphs again with the topic sentences in mind. You might be surprised at how rapidly comprehension increases.

46. Are there any other aids that might be used to improve reading skills?

Underlining key words and phrases helps, but a note of caution is needed here. A person unfamiliar with the skill of catching key words and phrases tends to underline too much. A paragraph littered with underlining can be so confusing as to be of no help to the student.

The reader should also look for unfamiliar words, circling or underlining them. Some of these words might be understood from the context in which they are used. Otherwise, the habit of using a dictionary should be developed.

It makes little difference whether speed or comprehension is stressed first. The two, as was pointed out earlier, go together. And once you acquire the skills involved in both, reading will become less difficult and much more rewarding.

Tips for better writing

Many people consider the ability to write well a gift, something a person either has or doesn't have. Certainly some people are more talented with the written word than others. But this doesn't mean that the average person can't learn to communicate on paper in clear, readable language. Given a desire to learn, guidance, patience, and practice, most students can learn to write just as they can learn most any other skill.

This is not to say that the task is easy. Few skills require as much practice as writing, and few are more susceptible to improvement. Almost everyone can write better. Furthermore, writing is a lonely task. Few pieces of good writing have been produced by committee.

On the other hand, good writing has its rewards. Not only can it help raise marks in school, but it also yields the personal satisfaction of having clearly conveyed an idea or information to a reader.

There are certain prerequisites to good writing, the first of which is to understand what one wants to say. If the writer doesn't understand, the reader never will.

Secondly, the writer must command an adequate vocabulary from which to select words to convey the meaning he or she intends. A good working vocabulary, like an ability to write, is not a gift. Everyone can accumulate one.

Third, good writing requires a familiarity with grammar, syntax, punctuation, and spelling. Mistakes in these areas stand out like neon signs.

You don't need to have a literary critic or an editor to help you learn to write better. Absorbing a few ideas about ordinary school requirements, about what is involved in the writing process, and reviewing some rules for good writing will prepare you sufficiently.

47. Why do teachers give so many written assignments?

This is a natural question students ask. It is a natural question because it involves a complaint heard from many students, especially from students to whom writing is a chore.

The answers to this question are quite simple. An ability to communicate on paper is a sign of education. Written assignments help develop both thinking skills and organizational skills. Also, such assignments mean practice and practice leads to improvement of writing skills. Furthermore, if a student must communicate on paper, he or she will tend to become more familiar with a subject and think about it harder. In this respect, a need to write becomes a stimulus to learning.

Moreover, one's success in school depends greatly on an ability to write. There are writing assignments for many courses. At the same time, examinations in many classes include essay questions. For such questions, skill in writing helps a student demonstrate that he or she knows an answer.

48. But doesn't a person need inspiration to write?

As any professional writer will tell you, the connection between inspiration and words on paper is flimsy at best. Any writer who waits for an inspiration before putting pencil to paper will get very little actual writing done. An assignment with a close deadline attached is a much sharper goad to writing. Few causes for harder thought and work exist.

49. What kinds of writing assignments might I run into?

Kinds of assignments vary, depending on subject and teacher. For the sake of discussion, though, writing assignments might be placed in either one of two categories. One category consists of writing based on personal experience. The other category leans mainly on sources outside the self.

Any kind of fiction, poetry, essay, or "how-to" piece based on one's own skill falls into the first classification. Sometimes this is called "informal writing."

A report on a book or an article, or on a topic requiring the use of more than one source, fits the second category. Sometimes this is called "formal writing." One type of writing requires slightly different skills than the other, but essentially all writing comes down to the skill of putting words on paper in a clear, concise, well-organized manner.

50. How should I select a topic for a writing assignment?

The student is usually totally devoid of ideas for a topic. Or, if he or she does have an idea for a topic, the student often fails to narrow it to manageable size.

Some teachers will allow you a great deal of room to maneuver when choosing a topic. Such teachers require only that the topic be within a particular area under study, for example the "Civil War" or "Insects." Other teachers will offer a list of topics within a broad range, allowing you to take your pick. Still others will be precise, and ask for "A report on the five points of the Treaty of Westphalia," perhaps even assigning the same topic to everyone in the class.

As to length, teachers usually specify a certain range in hundreds of words or number of pages. For example, some teachers will insist on essays that are no fewer than 400 or more than 500 words.

An open choice generates panic in many students. Their minds go blank. You can help yourself if you are willing to probe, listen, suggest, and stimulate yourself to zero in on a particular interest or area of knowledge. If the topic is to reflect personal experience, you might help by recalling some incident in your past, filling in details you might have forgotten or recall only dimly with information from your parents. Whatever the topic, it is important that it be narrowed so that it can be handled decently within a certain length.

Suggested topics themselves might actually prove too broad. A teacher might list "Health Foods" in a health class, "Weaving" in home economics, or "Democracy in Ancient Athens" in a history course. If you must produce an essay of 500 to 600 words—a typical length—any of these topics might prove unmanageable. You must try to pin health foods to a particular one, weaving to a particular kind, Athenian democracy to one or two aspects of it.

After selecting a topic from a list, you may find that there is not enough source material available to complete an essay. If this happens, an alternative topic must be chosen as quickly as possible. Ordinarily, though, teachers suggest topics for which material is readily available. There usually is little need to be concerned about not being able to locate information.

51. When is the best time to begin working on a writing assignment?

Immediately. Deadlines always seem far in the future at the beginning of a writing assignment. But suddenly, there they are. It is impossible to complete a writing assignment overnight and do a good job of it.

Beginning right away to think about an assignment establishes a receptivity to ideas. Even when you are not consciously thinking about a subject, the unconscious continues to operate. Ideas pop up when least expected; at bedtime, when sitting down to a meal, while walking down the street. You should be prepared to jot such ideas down as they occur.

And particularly with respect to "personal" pieces, those who teach writing would advise you to begin jotting ideas down long before you have all the thoughts you might wish to write about. The point is to get ideas down on paper. This procedure will usually generate other ideas. Probably much of the preliminary matter will be thrown away, but there often remains a gem or two worth polishing and building on.

52. What are the first steps in doing a typical writing assignment?

Because many school writing assignments concern reports, short or long, on some aspect of a subject the class has covered, we will use such a report as an example. Let's say the topic is "Adult Education." Such a topic might be a part of a history class, or a course in economics, or it might appear as a subject in a course dealing with contemporary trends or issues. Let us presume that you have been given an assignment to write a report of about 500 words on adult education.

It's a broad subject, involving evening programs for adults, adults returning to college, programs for retraining workers or having to do with hobbies, programs in which adults learn to read, and so on. Five thousand words or so might not do the subject justice. We must narrow the topic, identify some single aspect of it that could be covered adequately in 500 words.

A report dealing with "Adult Literacy Programs" might work. But this itself takes in a lot of territory—teaching techniques, learning materials, funding, sources of teachers, motivational problems, and other aspects. So this topic is also too broad. Suppose we zero in on the motivational problem, with the question "Why would adults want to learn to read?"

Once a possible topic has been identified, the next problem is to find source material from which to construct a report. Only a search in the library for books and articles will solve this problem. There is no other way.

Here the skill of scanning comes in handy. You can go through books and articles concerned with adult literacy programs, looking only for material on motivation, ignoring the rest.

Some communities sponsor special adult literacy programs. If that's true of your community, you might interview the director, some of the teachers involved in such a program and some of the clients. Such interviews can provide a wealth of information, and especially of human interest material.

As you uncover information, you should take notes. Each separate category of information should be recorded on half sheets of 8½ x 11 paper or on index cards. Each note should have a heading, so you can tell at a glance what the note is about. Having notes that refer to more than one heading on a card would cause trouble when you attempt to arrange the notes to fit some pattern of presentation.

53. How do I go about developing some sample headings for such a topic?

A typical heading on a note card being used to record research information for such a topic might be "obstacles to success." Under "obstacles to success" might be a note on the influence of failure in the past, another on lack of information about where to get help. "Lack of ambition, a cause" might be another heading, and "need for driver's license" another. We might have "economic betterment" and "examples of people who learned to read." And so on.

The point to be made again here is that each separate category of information must have its own note card or set of note cards. Otherwise, organization of the information into a coherent outline will take much more time than it normally should.

54. At what point should I begin organizing an outline?

Once a pattern seems to appear. This is the time to start outlining, or at least arranging the major points into categories. Some research will probably still remain to be done, but an outline will provide a framework that will guide your additional research. A brief outline for the topic "motivation for participation in adult literacy programs" might look like this:

    I. Introduction: extent of problem
   II. Programs to do something about it

III. Why people don't learn to read earlier
IV. Why adults avoid learning how to read
    A. past failure
    B. embarrassment
    C. "school is for kids" idea
V. How programs try to reach people
    A. TV and radio advertising
    B. student word of mouth
    C. personal contact by teachers and others
VI. In many cases, emphasis on getting better jobs
VII. Some people who have succeeded and why.

55. How should I prepare a first draft?

Research completed, notes assembled in order, you are now ready to try a first draft. The key to completing the first draft is starting it. This may sound strange. But even for many professional writers the most difficult task is to begin writing.

Putting the job off is the main enemy. You may tell yourself that since an outline and notes have been completed, the paper can be "dashed off" with no problem. While it may be possible to write some sort of paper on short notice, it is unlikely that a well-written paper can be done in this way.

You may have to discipline yourself to begin writing. Try to avoid criticism of your early attempts at a first draft. Results may be discouraging in the beginning. The idea is to keep trying, to keep reorganizing ideas and parts of the report, and to keep rewriting phrases and sentences until the flow of information begins to make sense.

Remember, the objective of the first draft is to get the paper into preliminary shape. You don't need to be overly careful about punctuation, grammar, and so on. However, while reviewing the first draft, you should note such errors. These errors will have to be corrected in the final draft of the paper.

Once you are satisfied that all necessary ideas have been put down on paper and that the flow of ideas makes sense, the first draft has been completed. The best thing to do now is to put the first draft aside for at least one full day. This will help you approach the next step in the writing of the paper with fresh ideas and fresh opinions.

56. How should I go about producing my final paper?

Basically, producing a final paper from a first draft involves revising that first draft. To revise means literally "to look again." Read that first draft. Remember, you probably will be as unfamiliar with the topic as any other person who will be reading the paper. If the content and flow of the first draft is difficult for you to understand, that is a good sign indicating substantial work remains to be done.

In the first draft you should have gotten the feel of the flow of the paper. In the revision, you should be aiming for consistency, continuity, precision, and power.

Do not be surprised if you find serious problems. Problems are to be expected. The idea is to catch and correct as many problems as possible at this point.

Perhaps the most common problem identified in a first draft is the presence of gaps in the flow of information. And one of the commonest gaps in student writing is the general summary statement that has no supporting data. Supporting data includes examples, reasons, arguments, details, and so on.

As you revise the first draft, look for expressions of opinion. Honestly ask yourself if there is enough evidence to convince a reader that this opinion is valid. Look for exaggerated statements, overstatements that are impossible to support.

After the gaps have been spotted, they should be filled in. Every generalization should be supported with convincing back-up data. The writer should add what a reader needs to know to make sense of the paper.

While you are adding necessary information to the paper, you should also be on the lookout for things that can be cut. If the assignment is for a 500 word paper, the final paper should be approximately 500 words in length, give or take perhaps five per cent. A 700 word paper in this situation could be as bad as a 300 word paper. The teacher may be trying to determine your ability to develop a topic concisely within a given limit as much as trying to find out how much you know about the given topic.

Read the paper again to see what needless parts can be cut. Look for unnecessary words. Often *who, which,* or *that* can be cut. Find short sentences that can be combined and words that can be cut as this is done. Avoid repetition. If repetition of ideas cannot be deleted entirely, change the wording of key sentences for the sake of variety.

57. What mistakes in writing should I work to avoid?

Grammar books have long defined a sentence as a subject completed by a verb, ordinarily ending with a period. "John fell" is as much a sentence as would be a construction containing more words relating how, why, and where he fell. The verb is the key; without a verb there is no sentence. That is why we consider such single words as "Run!" to be a sentence. The subject, "you," is understood.

Most sentences end with a period. But one or more can be separated by a comma; "He went to town, and he bought some groceries " Or by a semicolon: "The verb is the key; without a verb there is no sentence."

A question mark and an exclamation point can also end a sentence.

Avoid run-on sentences: "He walked home he forgot his book." Sometimes such sentences are incorrectly spliced together with a comma: "He walked home, he forgot his book."

Also avoid sentence fragments, sometimes called incomplete sentences. "He did not tell all he knew. Holding something back." "He did not have much time to get there. Plus his tiredness."

If you have problems with sentence structure, the best solution is practice. Reference to books of basic grammar may also be helpful. But the skill of constructing clear, concise, and correct sentences is one that is developed and sharpened by constant use.

Once you are satisfied with the structure of each sentence, study the paragraphs for coherence. Each paragraph should present a single idea and should hang together as a whole.

The central idea of each paragraph should be stated in a topic sentence. Go through the paper to determine what each paragraph is about. If there is no topic sentence, one that summarizes the message of the paragraph, one must be added.

Remember, a sentence is a group of words that are related. A paragraph is a group of sentences that are related. And a written assignment is a group of paragraphs that are related. All of these elements must "hang together" if the final paper is to make sense.

Sentences require subject and verb. And these two elements must agree in number (singular or plural). Singular subject, singular verb; plural subject, plural verb. To insure agreement simply ask the question, "who or what does what?" "The boy goes." "The boys go." And so on.

Students will write "The girls is walking to school" or "The girl are walking to school." Such errors are easy to catch. Difficulty arises when subject and verb are widely separated in a sentence. "The soldier with many medals along with his comrades were present at the ceremony." The word "comrades" can throw off the reader. "Was present" is what we want. Find the subject, then link it to the verb. "This flower, as well as the others, need water." Right or wrong?

The use of collective nouns can also cause a problem. "The group of students are ready." "The family were going." Both of these sentences are examples of errors in verb agreement. The sentences should read "group . . . is," and "family . . . is."

"None," "everyone," "no one"—students frequently assign plural verbs to these collective nouns. In fact, they take singular verbs.

Words taken directly from Latin can pose agreement problems. Is it "The data is" or "The data are?" "The media is," or "The media are?" "The strata is," or "The strata are?" The latter in each case. The singular form of these words is "datum," "medium," and "stratum."

In other cases, English usage has departed from strict adherence to Latin forms. We usually write "formulas" instead of "formulae" and "curriculums" instead of "curricula."

Pronouns must agree with their antecedents—the nouns to which they refer. "The girl raised her hand," "The girls raised their hands" seem simple enough. But what about "Everybody raise their hand?" No. It should be "Everybody raise his or her hand," just as "Each of the animals performed their trick well" should read "Each of the animals performed its trick well."

Students sometimes lose antecedents entirely. "The package was huge, with a flower tied to one side. It was blue." What does "it" refer to, package or flower? "The old house still stood, and a stone dog still guarded the gate. It was brown." Which, the dog or the gate?

Inexperienced writers tend to sprinkle their pieces with the indefinite "they." "They dig a lot of coal in Kentucky." "They say the world is coming to an end." "We were going to take the bus, but they would not let us." Who in the world is "they?" The good writer will be more specific.

Even though they have dealt with modifiers for years, junior and senior high school students still have trouble with adjectives and adverbs. The easiest rule is: adjectives modify nouns and pronouns, adverbs modify everything else. And, speaking generally, an adverb is a word that ends in "-ly." "He is skillful" (adjective). "He plays skillfully" (adverb).

However, there are exceptions to this rule. "Lovely" in "She is lovely" is an adjective, as it is in other cases. If you're speaking of state of mind or health, you say "He feels bad" not "He feels badly."

Misplaced modifying phrases probably cause inexperienced writers the most trouble. "They agreed when the temperature reached 100° to turn the machine off." Did "they" agree before the machine was started, or when the "temperature reached 100°?" More clear: "They agreed to turn the machine off when the temperature reached 100°." "Several people we know have gone that route." Does this mean we are acquainted with several people who "have gone that route?" Or does this mean we know that several people "have gone that route?"

Equally serious problems are dangling modifiers. "When getting into bed, his hand felt the object." ("His hand felt the object as he was getting into bed.") "Getting up from the floor, my toe hurt." ("I hurt my toe getting up from the floor.") "When looking into the room, the lamp fell over." ("The lamp fell over when I looked into the room.") You must constantly be on the lookout for these kinds of situations. Dangling modifiers can be pitfalls that turn into pratfalls. A writer must be on guard at all times.

The passive voice has some worthwhile functions. It comes in handy if the writer doesn't want to take or assign responsibility for a statement ("It is said that . . .") It is useful if the writer isn't quite sure of the facts. And the passive can lend variety to a paragraph.

On the whole, though, a good writer uses the passive sparingly. For one thing, it's much over-used. For another, it's weak and monotonous. Don't fall into the habit of relying on the passive voice. The active voice is more forceful, it is sharper, and its use tends to involve the reader.

Consider these sentences as constructed in the passive voice: "It was reported that the president was ill that day" (10 words). "It was voted to hold a banquet" (7 words). "After your record has been carefully examined and satisfaction still is lacking, it might be decided to let you go" (20 words). Recasting these sentences into the active voice we have: "The president was ill that day" (6 words); "We voted to hold a banquet" (6 words); and "Do your job or I might fire you" (8 words). Much better, and more economical.

58. What remains to be done to complete the writing assignment?

If you have not done it, compose an opening statement that tells the reader what the paper is all about. This "thesis statement" should be presented as early In the paper as possible.

In addition to beginning with an opening statement, the paper should end with a conclusion. The conclusion should cover the subject of the paper so well that a reader could get a good idea of the content of the entire paper just by reading the conclusion.

Most teachers prefer that papers be typed. The development of personal typing skills pays great dividends to any student. If you type the final paper, double spacing should be used.

You should leave a margin of 1½ inches on the left and approximately 1 inch on the other three sides, except for the first page. The first page of a written assignment is usually started 2 inches from the top.

If the paper is to be written longhand, single space should be used between sentences throughout. Double space should be used between paragraphs.

Finally, the paper should be proofread for typing or careless errors. The writing assignment is complete and ready to submit to the teacher.

Building a vocabulary

You need words. Words help you to communicate, to share your ideas and feelings with others. So expanding your vocabulary is a very practical thing for you to do.

The more words you know the more effectively you can speak, listen, read, write, and think. Words are the tools with which you think. And every idea you wish to communicate to others must be expressed in a language of some kind—words, painting, music, gestures, or signs. But mainly you communicate by using words. Therefore, the more words you know, the more ideas you can understand and share.

59. Why is vocabulary development important in school?

Your success in school is related to the size of your vocabulary. Students with the poorest vocabularies often get the poorest grades. Students with the best vocabularies often get the best grades.

You cannot understand a subject unless you know the key words in that subject. For example, the more key words you know in biology, the more you will be able to learn about that subject. If you do not know words such as legislative, executive, judicial, amendment, preamble, representative, and impeachment, you will not be able to understand much about the Constitution of the United States.

60. Does building my vocabulary mean learning big, hard words?

No. You need to increase the size of your vocabulary and become more skilled with words. But this does not always mean learning big, hard words. It means learning to use the exact words you need to explain your ideas to others. For example, the words *leave* and *abandon* have somewhat similar meanings. But there is a difference between *leaving* someone and *abandoning* someone. Is there a difference between an *uninterested* person and a *disinterested* person? You need the right word for the right occasion.

Choosing the right word is important. But keep in mind that words are not things. Words are symbols, something that stands for something else.

The word *chair* does not look like a *chair*. But to communicate effectively about the thing *chair*, you need to know the word, the symbol or the name for the thing *chair*.

Try to ask for a *chair* without using the word-symbol for *chair*. You will find yourself saying something like the following: "Please bring me a thing with four legs and a back that you sit on." Such a statement is both long and confusing. A listener could just as well interpret your request to be for a horse or camel as for a chair. So learning the names, the symbols, the words for things is a shortcut to more effective communication. And the more word-symbols you know how to use, the more exact will be the meaning of your communication.

But you still might say, "What good is it to learn words I may never use?" The answer to this question is simple. In school subjects, and in materials you will read in and out of school, you will meet many unfamiliar words. Whether you are in junior high school or a senior in college, you will still come across unfamiliar words. The larger your vocabulary is, the fewer the unfamiliar words you will be likely to encounter. And the fewer unfamiliar words you have to work with, the more efficient will be your reading and studying.

61. What are synonyms, and how do they help build vocabulary?

Synonyms are words that mean almost the same thing. Learning synonyms is a good way to build your vocabulary. It helps to organize words into groups. For example, under the idea of "little," you can mentally file such synonyms as *tiny, wee, minute, miniature, dwarf, elf,* and *pygmy.*

It is sometimes interesting to notice how many different synonyms there are for a word. How many synonyms can you think of for the word *prison?* Some are fancy words, some are down to earth: *house of correction, penal institution, penitentiary, jail, workhouse, dungeon, lockup, hoosegow, calaboose, jug, pokey,* and *clink.*

You can sharpen your vocabulary skills by learning the synonyms for common words. But you should also learn words that are dissimilar, words that have opposite meanings. Such words are called antonyms.

When you study antonyms, you begin to understand the relationships between words. If there is an *up*, there must be a *down*. If there is *light*, there must be *dark*. One idea does not exist without the other.

Therefore, when you learn a new word, it is a good idea to also learn its antonyms. It will not take long, and one word is easier to remember when you associate it with another. Some examples of words and their antonyms are:

male—female	*explode—implode*
masculine—feminine	*alpha—omega*
billygoat—nannygoat	*perigee—apogee*
buck—doe	*prologue—epilogue*

Notice that in studying word opposites you are making relationships between words and ideas. You are comparing and contrasting ideas. Thus, studying antonyms helps you see connections between opposite words such as

healthy—ailing	*sanitary—unsanitary*
sane—insane	*nutrition—malnutrition*
robust—frail	*immigrate—emigrate*

62. What are prefixes, and what do they have to do with vocabulary building?

Prefix means "something placed before" or, as a verb, "to put before." Prefixes can signal the meaning of words. And prefixes can serve as one key that can be used to unlock, or at least begin to define, a good many words. Let's look at a few common prefixes.

Take "anti-." It means "against" or "contrary." When you see a word beginning with the prefix "anti" you know immediately that you're dealing with something against or contrary to something else: *anti-*

aircraft, antibiotic, antihero, antimatter, antislavery, antipathy.

Don't mix "anti-" up with "ante-," though. "Ante-" indicates before: *antecedent, antechamber, antedate.*

"Bi-" is another common prefix, meaning two: *bicentennial, bicep, bicolor, bicycle, biennial, bifocal.* "Pre" (as in prefix) also means before: *prearrange, pre-Columbian, preschool, preamble, prelude.*

"Ex," meaning "out of" or "from," is yet another common prefix: *exclaim, exhaust, exit.* And we also have "super," which means "above" or "to place over" or "superior": *supermarket, supernatural, supercede, superscription, superstructure.* And, as another, there is "post," meaning "after": *postnasal, postnatal, postwar, post meridian, postlude, postpone.*

Lists of common prefixes can be found in many dictionaries, grammar books, and books dealing with language and usage. Work to familiarize yourself with common prefixes. They are an important aid to vocabulary building.

63. What are suffixes and how do they help in the work of vocabulary building?

As with prefixes, the more suffixes—or word endings—a person knows, the more word meanings he or she has at his or her command. And this means a larger vocabulary.

"Able" and "ible," meaning "possible to do," are examples—and whether one or the other should be used sometimes causes problems that only a dictionary can solve. We have *readable, manageable, capable, changeable, attainable;* and we also have *credible, edible, legible, tangible, susceptible.*

The suffixes "ant" and "ent" refer to "person who." And they too can cause spelling mixups. It's *immigrant, defendant, participant, informant, attendant;*

and *president, referent, resident, dependent, correspondent*. The suffix "orium" refers to "the place where": *auditorium* (where we listen), *natatorium* (where we swim), and *emporium* (where we trade or shop).

Like prefixes, common suffixes are listed in many sources. And, as with prefixes, you should familiarize yourself with the more commonly used suffixes.

64. Are prefixes and suffixes the same as root words?

No! Basically, a root is something to which a prefix or suffix may be added, although a root can also be a word in its own right. This is especially true of root words derived from another language. The Greek words "homo" (same) and "autos" (self) are examples of this. From the word "homo" we have *homocentric, homogeneous, homograph, homonym, homozygous,* and many other words. From the word "autos" we obtain *automobile, autograph, autobiography,* and *autohypnotism*.

"Graph," meaning "write," is a root appearing as a suffix. And you can see that some of the words above represent a joining of roots—for example, "auto" plus "graph" (self-write).

"Agr"—land or soil—is another common root, giving us *agriculture, agronomy, agribusiness, agrostology, agrimony,* and so on. Still another we see quite a bit of is "annu"—year—as in *annual, annuity, anniversary, superannuate,* and *annuitant*.

A working knowledge of root words is not easy to achieve. It takes time, care, and attention. But it is a task that is well worth the effort. Because of the extensive use of root words in the English language, each root word you learn becomes a foundation upon which a major expansion of vocabulary may be built.

65. How will a dictionary help me build my vocabulary?

A dictionary is probably the single most important tool you can use to build your vocabulary. A dictionary is primarily a list of words, their spelling, and their meaning. Use of a dictionary will help you to learn new words, and to refine the meanings and uses of words you already know.

66. What kind of information can I find in a dictionary?

When you research a topic, you need a resource, something that contains information. The dictionary is a word resource. It can tell you many things about a word, such as meaning, spelling, and pronunciation. And the dictionary can also tell you about the origin and history of a word.

A dictionary can help you choose the right word for the right occasion. It can help you to better understand the shade of difference in the meaning of similar words.

67. How are the word entries in many dictionaries arranged?

Entry words are the main words or head words in a dictionary. There are several important facts about word entries that you should know.

Main entry words are listed in large, boldface type. These main entry words are listed in strict alphabetical order.

Different spellings of the same word may be listed together; for example, **usable,** also **useable.** They may also be listed as separate entry words; for example, **amoeba** or **ameba.**

Finally, main entries may be single words, compound words, phrases, abbreviations, prefixes, suffixes, or root words. A thorough understanding of the arrangement and uses of main entry words is vital to the proper use of a dictionary. While considering these features, it would probably be helpful to have a dictionary close by. Constant reference to actual main entry words should clarify any questions you may have.

68. What other features do many dictionaries have?

While main entry words are the basic component of a dictionary, there are many other features. Each set of facing pages containing word entries has a guide word on each outside top corner. The guide word on the left-hand page indicates what the first entry on the set of facing pages is. The guide word on the right-hand page indicates what the last entry on the set of facing pages is. Use of guide words will help you find entries quickly and easily.

A dictionary is also a grammar resource. A dictionary entry includes what part of speech a word is. And a dictionary will show you how a word may be used in a phrase or sentence. Parts of speech are listed in alphabetical order, adjective first, then noun, then verb.

A dictionary contains information on the etymology, the original meaning or derivation, of a word or its parts. This is often helpful in understanding the exact meaning of the word.

A dictionary as a source for synonyms and antonyms is especially important. If you look up a word in the dictionary and do not understand the definition, you can look at the synonyms and antonyms for the word and probably find some that are familiar. These will provide clues to the meaning of the word originally looked up.

A dictionary gives hints about word usage, the grammatically proper use of certain words. Usage notes in a dictionary will help you to be grammatically correct in your use of words.

As part of the information on usage, a dictionary often explains the use of colloquialisms, words used in everyday, informal speech. And it often includes slang; flashy, popular words used in a special way.

Many words have more than one meaning. Such words can be used in many different senses. A dictionary usually lists all the valid meanings for a word. This feature can help you increase your vocabulary. Extending vocabulary is not only a question of learning new words. It is also a matter of extending the number of meanings you can attach to a word you already know. And a dictionary can help you to do this.

69. What is a thesaurus, and how may it be used?

A thesaurus is a collection of synonyms and antonyms for commonly used words. As in a dictionary, main entry words are arranged in alphabetical order, followed by a list of all appropriate synonyms and antonyms.

Any student who must prepare written assignments should have access to a thesaurus. And so should any student who is interested in building his or her vocabulary.

70. Can metaphor be used to aid vocabulary building?

Of course. You should experiment with words and play with words. Many of our most commonly used expressions come from trying out words in different situations. Words are elastic, and people can stretch the meanings of words. This process is called making metaphors. For example, you may describe someone as "having a heart of stone." Obviously, the person's heart is not really stone. But it is compared to stone. A metaphor has been used.

Look for metaphors in the newspapers. Listen for them on the radio and television. And try to notice how often you use metaphors. This will help you to learn new words by playing with words.

71. Are there any other techniques that will help me to build a larger vocabulary?

Yes! Another way to learn new words by playing with words is by noticing their construction. Games such as crossword puzzles will require you to look closely at how a word is spelled and how the letter of one word blends into another word.

You might try to work anagrams. These are word games in which one word is changed into another word by moving the letters. One example of an anagram is are—ear.

Finally, a word game that is difficult and challenging is the construction of palindromes. Palindromes are words or phrases that read the same backward or forward. Good examples of palindromes are *level*, *radar*, and *gold log*.

The use of such techniques can be a great deal of fun. And, at the same time, use of such techniques can have an important educational payoff in increased understanding of the meaning and use of words.

72. How does all this help the job of vocabulary building?

By this point it should be clear that vocabulary building is not a simple matter of the memorization of lists of words and their definitions. Vocabulary building is not like other educational skills that must be acquired.

Vocabulary building is a long-term proposition that involves the creation of an attitude of curiosity about words, and a desire to use the correct word in the correct situation. Through the use of the information, tools, and techniques described in this chapter you can, hopefully, develop such an attitude and desire. Above all, building in this case involves using.

Finally, keep in mind the fact that vocabulary building is a process that should continue past the period of formal education. By learning and practicing techniques of vocabulary development, you will be investing in a process that will pay you rich dividends for the rest of your life.

73. How can I determine my present vocabulary level?

This information is necessary in helping you to evaluate your word skill level. Such information will give you a clue as to what and how much work is to be done in the area of vocabulary development.

As an aid to determining your present word skill level, we have included the following three exercises. **Exercise A** includes terms that are appropriate for the upper elementary school student; **Exercise B,** for the junior high student; **Exercise C,** for the senior high student. Choose the appropriate exercise, complete it on a sheet of paper, and score it using the appropriate answer key. A score of 50 per cent or more wrong would indicate that extensive vocabulary development work is needed.

Exercise A

Complete each sentence by choosing the correct

word from the choices that have been provided.
Correct answers are at the end of the word quiz.

1. A DON'T WALK sign means you are _____ to cross the street.
   a. allowed   b. reminded   c. forbidden

2. He offered a _____ about how to prepare for a bike hike.
   a. suggestion   b. donation   c. question

3. The astronauts _____ from their capsule to the orbiting spaceship.
   a. rescued   b. transferred   c. separated

4. A person who commits a crime must pay the _____.
   a. cost   b. amount   c. penalty

5. A person who does not know what to do should get _____.
   a. ready   b. confused   c. advice

6. The shortening of a word is called an _____.
   a. abbreviation   b. accent   c. adjustment

7. The Pilgrims left England and formed a _____ in America.
   a. territory   b. nation   c. colony

8. The _____ is the line where the sky and earth appear to meet.
   a. atmosphere   b. equator   c. horizon

9. The subject matter of a book arranged alphabetically is called the _____.
   a. preface   b. contents   c. index

10. _____ means dealing fairly with everyone.
    a. Freedom   b. Liberty   c. Justice

11. In the word *submarine, sub* is a _____.
    a. suffix   b. root   c. prefix

12. The area near the North Pole is called the _____ Zone.
    a. Tropic   b. Arctic   c. Torrid

13. An _____ machine works by itself.
    a. oiled   b. automatic   c. operated

14. You use a _____ to find direction.
    a. barometer   b. altimeter   c. compass
15. The letters D, K, and T are called _____.
    a. abbreviations   b. consonants   c. vowels
16. The _____ is an imaginary line around the earth,
    equally distant from the North and South poles.
    a. latitude   b. equator   c. longitude
17. It is hard to walk on ice because there is little
    _____ between your feet and the ice.
    a. contact   b. gravity   c. friction
18. Heat is one form of _____.
    a. fuel   b. gas   c. energy
19. A _____ is a person from another country.
    a. native   b. foreigner   c. citizen
20. To rule or control a country is to _____ it.
    a. free   b. establish   c. govern
21. A _____ to drive a car gives you permission to
    drive it.
    a. ticket   b. sticker   c. license
22. _____ is doing something often so you can do it
    well.
    a. Work   b. Recreation   c. Practice
23. _____ holds us onto the earth's surface.
    a. Friction   b. Gravity   c. Weight
24. A _____ is a meaningful syllable at the end of
    a word.
    a. prefix   b. root   c. suffix
25. To put off doing something until later is to
    _____ it.
    a. forget   b. reject   c. postpone

Answers: 1.c, 2.a, 3.b, 4.c, 5.c, 6.a, 7.c, 8.c, 9.c, 10.c,
11.c, 12.b, 13.b, 14.c, 15.b, 16.b, 17.c, 18.c, 19.b, 20.c,
21.c, 22.c, 23.b, 24.c, 25.c.

Exercise B

Complete each sentence by choosing the correct word

from the choices that have been provided. Correct answers are at the end of the word quiz.

1. A *dispatch* is an official _____.
   a. message   b. command   c. speech
2. A _____ is a pipe that carries hot air from a furnace to a room.
   a. pump   b. blower   c. duct
3. A person who feels great bliss or joy is _____.
   a. romantic   b. in ecstasy   c. in a trance
4. _____ persons do their jobs with skill.
   a. Efficient   b. Conscientious   c. Sincere
5. To sew in designs on cloth is to _____ the cloth.
   a. knit   b. embroider   c. crochet
6. Customary rules of behavior in polite society are called _____.
   a. manners   b. ordinances   c. etiquette
7. If you try hard, you are _____ yourself.
   a. forcing   b. exerting   c. overtaxing
8. Judges in court dispense or _____ justice.
   a. inspire   b. recommend   c. administer
9. *Anthropology* means _____.
   a. love of mankind   b. study of man
   c. having human form
10. The *blockade* of a port by ships _____ the port.
    a. clears   b. controls   c. opens
11. When she decided not to take the plane, she _____ her reservation.
    a. requested   b. made   c. canceled
12. The opposite of *simple* is _____.
    a. solemn   b. sincere   c. complex
13. A *decade* is _____.
    a. an athletic event   b. a geometric figure
    c. a ten-year period
14. _____ is getting rid of a problem.
    a. Discussion   b. Elimination   c. Agreement
15. Money paid out is called _____.
    a. credits   b. receipts   c. expenditures

84

16. If you gain something by deceit, the judge may find you guilty of _____.
    a. dishonesty   b. fraud   c. trickery
17. In a theater the *gallery* is the _____ balcony.
    a. lowest   b. middle   c. highest
18. A *hypocrite* _____.
    a. is very critical   b. imagines he's ill
    c. is a false person
19. A sudden desire to do something is an _____.
    a. impulse   b. impact   c. instigation
20. Some scientists believe space is endless. It has _____ boundaries.
    a. defined   b. infinite   c. definite
21. A red swelling on the body is _____.
    a. an inflammatory   b. an inflammable
    c. an inflammation
22. If a dead relative leaves you his house, you _____ it.
    a. occupy   b. annex   c. inherit
23. *Ex* (out) + *clude* (shut) = *exclude*, meaning _____.
    a. shut in   b. shut out   c. shut up
24. *Psychology* is the study of the _____.
    a. mind   b. body   c. spirit
25. Depending on the pronunciation, the word *invalid* has two meanings. What are they?
    _____ _____.
    a. of no value   b. priceless   c. a sick person

Answers: 1.*a*, 2.*c*, 3.*b*, 4.*a*, 5.*b*, 6.*c*, 7.*b*, 8.*c*, 9.*b*, 10.*b*, 11.*c*, 12.*c*, 13.*c*, 14.*b*, 15.*c*, 16.*b*, 17.*c*, 18.*c*, 19.*a*, 20.*b*, 21.*c*, 22.*c*, 23.*b*, 24.*a*, 25.*a,c*.

Exercise C

Complete each sentence by choosing the correct word from the choices that have been provided. Correct answers are at the end of the word quiz.

1. _____ speeds up your heartbeat.
   a. Anesthesia   b. Analgesic   c. Adrenalin
2. _____ describes a deep, dark, seemingly bottom-less hole in the earth.
   a. Fissure   b. Abyss   c. Opaque
3. _____ nerves deal with the sense of hearing.
   a. Cerebral   b. Optic   c. Auditory
4. To give praise unwillingly is to _____ it.
   a. begrudge   b. withhold   c. retain
5. The surgical removal of tissue from a living body is called _____.
   a. autopsy   b. pathology   c. biopsy
6. In ancient times a _____ was used to hurl stones.
   a. battering ram   b. crossbow   c. catapult
7. The _____ is the frame, wheels, machinery, and running gear of an automobile.
   a. body   b. chassis   c. assembly
8. To _____ is to figure or calculate.
   a. compute   b. compensate   c. comprise
9. A _____ statement is scornful.
   a. conflicting   b. contradicting
   c. contemptuous
10. _____ may be described as rage or violent anger.
    a. Madness   b. Wrath   c. Rivalry
11. When a person says one thing and does another it destroys his _____.
    a. credulity   b. credentials   c. credibility
12. Fine glassware is called _____.
    a. china   b. crystal   c. porcelain
13. The _____ carries out the provisions of a will.
    a. bequeather   b. recipient   c. executor
14. A _____ often involves continual talking to delay the passing of a law.
    a. caucus   b. filibuster   c. quorum
15. The chemical compound _____ is applied to the teeth to decrease decay.
    a. chlorine   b. fluoride   c. phosphate

16. The _____ are the "cutting" teeth.
    a. molars   b. biscuspids   c. incisors
17. The Washington Monument, a tall, single, four-sided stone, is an example of _____.
    a. an epitaph   b. a mausoleum   c. an obelisk
18. A _____ is a five-angled, five-sided figure.
    a. hexagon   b. pentagon   c. heptagon
19. The word _____ means a long, adventurous journey.
    a. sojourn   b. wayfarer   c. odyssey
20. The last letter of the Greek alphabet is _____.
    a. alpha   b. delta   c. omega
21. An _____ disaster is one that is likely to happen soon.
    a. disputable   b. indubitable   c. impending
22. An _____ speech is done without preparation.
    a. impulsive   b. impromptu   c. impetuous
23. A _____ disease directly affects the lungs.
    a. vascular   b. neurological   c. pulmonary
24. The word _____ refers to the withdrawal of the Southern states from the Union.
    a. recession   b. secession   c. concession
25. The words _____ and _____ both mean *eggs*.
    a. yegg   b. ova   c. roe

Answers: 1.c, 2.b, 3.c, 4.a, 5.c, 6.c, 7.b, 8.a, 9.c, 10.b, 11.c, 12.b, 13.c, 14.b, 15.b, 16.c, 17.c, 18.b, 19.c, 20.c, 21.c, 22.b, 23.c, 24.b, 25.b,c.

Finding information

Handed a writing assignment, a student often panics twice. The first panic occurs when he or she is faced with finding a topic. Once a topic has been chosen, another panic sets in—where will resource material be found?

The obvious answer—as everyone knows—is in the library. Yet, for a surprisingly large number of students, telling them to use a library is like suggesting that they venture into a foreign and forbidden land. They either don't know the first thing about using a library, or they're not sufficiently aware of the many resources and aids a library offers.

At some time during your school career, you probably had some instruction in how to use a library. Perhaps this instruction came in a language arts class or in an English class. In most schools, though, this library instruction is very minimal, and the degree of rub-off varies greatly among students.

However, as a student progresses in school, library

resources become more and more important and valuable. Virtually every student could benefit from a refresher course in how to use the library. And that is what we hope to provide in this chapter.

74. How is the information contained in libraries organized?

Libraries classify and catalog books and other source material according to a combination of numbers and letters. And if you've ever tried to find information in a book without an index, you realize how valuable an asset a library classification system is.

All libraries have what is called a card catalog. This is composed of 3" × 5" cards filed in long narrow boxes. Each card contains information about one book. Each book has an author card, which catalogs a book by author; a title card, which catalogs a book by title; and a subject card, which catalogs a book by general topic.

If you are looking for a particular book, you will probably know the name of the author and/or the book's title. You may then look in the card catalog—arranged alphabetically—under the author's last name or the first word of the title (excluding "the," "an," and "and"). Some libraries have a separate card catalog for authors and titles. Other libraries mix author and title cards.

For the person looking for a particular book, the most important information appears at the upper left-hand corner of the card, the combination of numbers and letters known as the "call number." More about the call number later.

75. How do I go about locating information in a library?

In this event you should look for subject headings. The subject cards may or may not be kept separate from the author and title cards. This makes no difference; the procedure in either case is the same.

Subject cards have headings in capital letters to distinguish them from author or title cards. Principal headings might be Europe, History; Far East, History; United States, History; or Physics, Botany, Biology. These in turn are broken down into subheadings; for example, Physics, Atomic or Physics, Space. United States and other history categories appear chronologically, for example:

U.S.—History—Discovery and Exploration
U.S.—History—Colonial Period
U.S.—History—Revolutionary War
U.S.—History—Constitution
U.S.—History—War of 1812
U.S.—History—Civil War
U.S.—History—1920–1929

And so on. If you wanted material on the westward movement, though, you would look not under U.S. History, but under Westward Movement, U.S. If the subject was economic depression, material would be found under Panics, Financial, U.S.

A subject card contains the same information as an author or a title card. There is one addition—the subject indicated in capital letters at the top of the card.

One book can, of course, be found under several subject headings. A volume on the westward movement before the Civil War might be found listed under U.S.—History—1820–1850 and under Westward Movement, U.S. as well.

When you have located a title that appears promising, then the call number becomes important. Nonfiction books are shelved according to call number, running from the lowest to the highest. With your call number in hand, you may go to the appropriate place on the shelves where the book should be.

76. How do libraries classify and number books?

There are two major systems of classification. One is the Dewey Decimal System, the other the Library of Congress System. Most libraries use one or the other; some use both.

The Dewey Decimal System dates from 1876. At that time Melvil Dewey completed his task of establishing ten categories of subjects, to which he assigned numbers from 000 to 999. The ten divisions are:

000–999—General Works (encyclopedias, bibliographies, periodicals, journalism)
100–199—Philosophy, Psychology, Ethics
200–299—Religion and Mythology
300–399—Social Sciences (economics, sociology, government, law, education, vocations, customs)
400–499—Philology (language, dictionaries, grammar)
500–599—Science (mathematics, astronomy, physics, chemistry, geology, paleontology, biology, zoology, botany)
600–699—Useful Arts (medicine, engineering, agriculture, home economics, business, radio, television, aviation)
700–799—Fine Arts (architecture, sculpture, painting, music, photography, recreation)
800–899—Literature (novels, poetry, plays, criticism)
900–999—History, Geography, Biography, Travel

Librarians assign numbers within each of these ranges to subjects that fall under the main headings. Within 600–699, the "useful arts," numbers 600–639 refer to agriculture. Agricultural subjects are then sub-divided into such categories as field crops, garden crops, dairy products, and insects related to agriculture.

The term "decimal system" refers to the fact that subdivisions are further broken down according to numbers appearing to the right of a decimal point following the main three numbers. For example, books on useful insects come under 638. Those on beekeeping would be under 638.1, those on silk-worms, 638.2. As another example, a book might bear the call number 796.32. Translated, this would become 7 (the arts), 9 (recreation), 6 (games), 3 (with a ball), and 2 (that's thrown). This might be any one of a number of games. Actually, it's basketball; foot-ball, baseball, and other games with balls have dif-ferent numbers to the right of the decimal point.

Below this number will be a capital letter followed by a number and perhaps a lower-case letter. For example, a book on New England Puritans by John Fiske appears as

973.2

F 547b

The lower line refers to the author, and is called a Cutter number.

77. What is the Library of Congress Classification System?

This is a more precise classification system than the Dewey Decimal Classification System. The Library of Congress Classification System is useful to such large libraries as the Library of Congress and libraries located at universities. Instead of ten broad subjects, the Library of Congress, or LC, system uses twenty-one.

This is the breakdown:

A   General Works
B   Philosophy, Psychology, and Religion
C, D, E, F   History
G   Geography, Anthropology, and Recreation
H   Social Sciences
J   Political Science
K   Law
L   Education
M   Music
N   Fine Arts
P   Language and Literature
Q   Science
R   Medicine
S   Agriculture
T   Technology
U   Military Science
V   Naval Science
Z   Bibliography and Library Science

An LC call number might look like this:

QL116
.J25

Translated, this would be Q (Science), L (zoology, a subdivision), 116 (deserts), .J25 (author number). The call number refers to a book by Edmund Carroll Jaeger on the subject of *Desert Wildlife*.

These symbols, whether drawn from the Dewey Decimal, the LC, or some other system, appear on the book's spine. And the books are shelved beginning with 000 and ending with 999.

78. What about works of fiction?

Under the Dewey System, classical English and non-English fiction, translated or not, would be found in the 800-899 category. More modern fiction written in English, according to Dewey, is classified according to the first letter of the author's last name. The card catalog will tell you whether the library has a particular work of fiction. But since many authors have the same first letter in their last names, it might take a little time to track the book down alphabetically on the shelves.

The LC System classifies fiction under P, Language and Literature, assigning a second letter to designate country of origin. The first two letters for American fiction are PS.

79. Is all this information about cataloging systems really of much help to the general library user?

Certainly it's more valuable to the professional cataloger. Yet it might be useful for you to know about the systems, particularly if your library uses both systems. In that case, you might come up with two totally different types of call numbers for two books on the same subject.

Also, there may be times when you will want to get a general idea of a library's holdings in a particular subject, or times when a student is simply browsing. Then a knowledge of what classification symbols mean can be useful. If you know that 973 refers to United States history, a "cruise through the stacks" will tell you how useful that library might be if you are interested in that subject.

80. Are there any "tricks" to using a card catalog?

There are a few things to keep in mind beyond the fact that the cards are arranged alphabetically. For example, abbreviations are considered to be written out, even if they are abbreviated in the title of the book: look for Doctor, Saint, and Mister, not for Dr., St., and Mr. And anyone who uses a card catalog probably wishes there were no such names as McDuff and Macdonald. One must remember that "mc" and "mac" are filed as though they were all "mac," and run in with other words beginning with M. So we have

McAdam, Henry	Machinery
Macadamia nuts	McLean, Alan
Macbeth	McLean, John
McHenry	Macmillan, Thomas

Watch for cross-references when using subject cards. Sometimes the card will indicate that you are looking under the wrong heading—CARS, see AUTOMOBILE, for instance. Then, frequently at the end of a number of cards on a subject there might be a card suggesting that you "see also"—AUTOMOBILE, see also ASSEMBLY LINE, ELECTRIC, HENRY FORD, STEAM, and so on.

One further point. Works *by* a person come before works *about* a person. And those about a person will have a heading in all capital letters. So, Fiske, John, *The Beginnings of New England* will precede the heading JOHN FISKE, under which might be listed Appel, George, *John Fiske and American Historiography*.

81. What if the book or other piece of material I need is not on the shelf?

You should be aware that this is a common experience. However, there are several things that can be done.

The item you are searching for might be in the wrong place, so check to the right and to the left, up and down. Or it might be on a table or a study desk. Check there. If the item still cannot be found, you should check with the people at the circulation desk. Many libraries now have computer systems that enable them to track down an item immediately—it's checked out, or lost, strayed, or stolen, or it's in the bindery for repair.

If the item has been checked out, you might just have to wait until it's returned, although you can be put on a list to be notified when that happens.

If an item has been out beyond a certain time period, but is not quite due, you might be able to have it called in especially for you, within a week, perhaps.

Should an item be lost, strayed, or stolen—and this might not be known for sure until the library has searched for a couple of weeks—all is not lost. Most libraries participate in an interlibrary loan service. You furnish the author and title and within a couple of weeks your library will obtain the book or other item for you from another participating library.

82. Does a library's card catalog list all the books that may be available for any given subject area?

Only with respect to that particular library. To discover the titles of other books that might be useful, you should consult *Books in Print* and *Paperbound Books in Print*, copies of which most libraries carry. These reference works are arranged both by author and title and by subject. They represent the most complete lists available on books currently carried and for sale by publishers. With author and title in hand from one of these sources, you can check at another library in your vicinity—for example, the town public library if you have been concentrating on your school library. If you still need other books, then you can request additional materials through the interlibrary loan service.

83. What other sources of information might a library hold?

A great many. One research tool you should direct your attention to is the *Readers' Guide to Periodical Literature*. This source, going back to the turn of the century in origin, is the most up-to-date and complete compilation of articles published in selected major periodicals. The *Readers' Guide* doesn't list *every* article published in every periodical each year, but it certainly lists enough to satisfy most researchers.

To indicate a little of what *Readers' Guide* contains, here is a section from the China entry in the volume covering March 1977 to February 1978:

Moral conditions
Back door: illicitly obtained goods and services.
 Time 111:24 Ja 9 '78
S-e-x, H. Jensen and S. Liu. il Newsweek 91:
 48–9 Ja 16 '78

Nationalism
Ethnic relations in China. J. T. Dreyer. bibl
 Ann Am Acad 433: 100–11 S '77

Politics and Government
China after Mao. O. E. Clubb. bibl Cur Hist 73:
 49:53 | S '77
China ends an era. A. Deming and Others. Il
 Newsweek 90:32–33+ Ag 29 '77
Comeback for Teng? K. Willenson and others. por
 Newsweek 89:51 Ja 24 '77

Eternal China, eternal conspiracies. R. Elegant.
il map Nat R 29:1167+ O 14 '77

Legacy of the Gang of Four. Time 110:46 N 7 '77

Reading Chinese tea leaves. S. E. Crane. Common-
weal 104:393–7 Je 24 '77

Second comeback for Comrade Teng. il pors Time
110:23–4 Ag 1 '77

Teng: China's real boss. M. Smith. il por Newsweek
90:43–4 S 12 '77

Thought control in Mao's China: interview with
Chinese intellectual. ed. by W. Berkson. Nat R
29:1173–7+O 14 '77

Was Chou murdered? F. Willey and others. il por
Newsweek 89:49 F 7 '77

Welcome home: T. Hsiao-ping. il por Newsweek 90:
34 Ag 1 '77

Wide of the mark. C. Johnson. New Repub 177:12–
14 N 26 '77

See also: **Communism—China**

Religious institutions and affairs
Where have all the churches gone? J. B. Wang. Chr
Today 22:12–13 N 18 '77

See also: **Catholic Church in China, Christians in China**

Each issue of the *Readers' Guide* includes an expla-
nation of the abbreviations. We will, however, trans-
late those that might not seem familiar in the quoted
section above. The first part of the entry is the article's
title, followed by the name of the author, if it is
given. Then the title of the periodical is given (Ann
Am Acad: *Annals of the American Academy;* Cur
Hist: *Current History;* Nat R: *National Review;* New
Repub: *New Republic;* Chr Today: *Christianity Today*).
Next we have the issue's volume number, followed
by page numbers, then the month or the day of the
month and the year. Other abbreviations include,
"il": illustrated; "bibl": bibliography; "por": either

pictures of an individual or a character sketch; and "il map": illustrated with a map.

By following subject headings, subheadings, and cross-references, you can find any number of periodical articles related to the subject you are researching. The only way to determine if articles are really useful, of course, is to examine each individually; titles do not always give the complete picture. To find out if a library carries a specific periodical, you must consult a list found in each library's reference room. If the library doesn't have a certain periodical, or a certain issue, most libraries will obtain a photocopy of the desired piece from another library.

84. What other reference works that most libraries have might I find useful?

Most libraries have a large number of reference works you should know about. Among encyclopedias there are *The World Book Encyclopedia, The Encyclopedia Americana,* and *The New Encyclopaedia Britannica in 30 Volumes.* Geographic information may be found in an atlas, which contains maps and some statistical data; in gazetteers, which hold considerable statistical information; and in dictionaries of geography. Records and other statistics, both historical and recent, can be found in such sources as *The World Almanac and Book of Facts* and *Information Please Almanac; Atlas and Yearbook,* both published on an annual basis. In the "how-to" category there are various volumes dealing with such topics as home repairs, gardening, and construction techniques.

Current Biography is a monthly publication dealing with people currently on the scene, and there are numerous volumes of historical biographies. Names and addresses can be found in directories of professions and associations, and in telephone directories from various cities. Many libraries carry these items. Finally, there are bibliographies of all kinds, listing titles of books on various subjects and categories of subjects.

85. What about reference works dealing with specific subjects?

There is almost no end to these. Consult your librarian and the card catalog. But here is a sampling: *The Negro Almanac, The Encyclopedia of Military History: from 3500 B.C. to the Present, New Rhyming Dictionary and Poets' Handbook, A Dictionary of Contemporary American Usage, A Dictionary of Slang and Unconventional English, The New Space Encyclopaedia: A Guide to Astronomy and Space Exploration, The Baseball Encyclopedia: The Complete and Official Record of Major League Baseball,* and *Atlas of the American Revolution.* This list barely scratches the surface.

86. Are there any words of caution about using reference works?

If you are looking for recent statistics, be sure to check the date of the reference work. A *World Almanac,* for example, will contain facts from the year before the date appearing on the cover. The *Almanac* for 1979 will cover the events up to and including the year 1978.

The same holds true for encyclopedias. Some, like *The World Book Encyclopedia,* undergo annual revision of substantial portions. Others go for years with little or no revision. Facts, maps, and other information can quickly get out of date. Check the copyright dates.

The latest copyright date listed will indicate the year in which the volume was published.

Some encyclopedias publish yearbooks, such as *The World Book Year Book*. These, like almanacs, are up to date for the year previous to that appearing on the cover.

87. What happens if you find conflicting information in two different reference works?

This can happen. Two encyclopedias, two almanacs, might contain conflicting dates for an event, conflicting geographic information, and so forth. If you run into this, you should check a third source, if possible. If a third source of information cannot be located, the best you can do is to cite both sources of the information, calling attention to the point in conflict.

88. What about the use of newspapers as sources of information?

These, of course, are excellent for current events. But newspapers should be used with caution, for newspapers are produced against tight deadlines, and errors do creep in.

In many cases, a library's newspaper holdings are on microfilm. And it might be possible to obtain film copies of newspapers your library doesn't have from other libraries.

The New York Times regularly publishes an extensive index, which is extremely valuable in tracking down news stories, features, and editorials. If a library doesn't collect the *Times*, interlibrary loans of microfilmed copies are available. In addition, the *Times* index can be used to get the dates of stories, accounts of which might then be located in a local or other available newspaper.

89. Are there sources of useful information outside the sources available in libraries?

Indeed there are. Depending on the topic, the personal interview may be one such source. Suppose, for example, that you are writing a paper on small business people and their problems. Every community has a number of small business people, and personal interviews can uncover much valuable and intimate information. Information obtained through interviews is often of a kind unobtainable from a book, a newspaper or magazine article, or a government report.

Personal surveys are another means of getting information. Such surveys, however, are difficult to carry out. A questionnaire must be developed, distributed, and collected. This takes time and effort, and results can be disappointing. But if successful, reports based on personal surveys can be interesting. Reports or papers that have to do with opinions, habits, attitudes, and the like readily lend themselves to the use of surveys.

You can also gain information from television and radio programs. In some instances you can obtain summaries, study guides, and bibliographies of research sources for many programs by writing to a local station or to the network. Such programs can be especially valuable for topics that deal with current problems and events.

90. What about government documents?

Local, state, and federal governments publish thousands of documents, special reports, surveys, and so forth each year. To track down what is needed, you should consult catalogs of government publications. These catalogs can be found in many libraries.

Taking tests

Tests, like death and taxes, are always with us. And tests do not end with graduation from the system of formal education. You might leave the written variety behind, but most people are tested every day in one way or another. This is particularly true in the work people do to earn a living. Although you may not realize it now, we all must meet requirements and we all must perform.

You, of course, are mainly concerned with the pencil and paper tests you encounter in practically every course in school. These range from hastily drawn, quick daily quizzes to the formidable appearing, printed standardized tests that measure achievement, fitness for a vocation or college, and ability.

Naturally, the person who has studied thoroughly is better prepared and should feel more at ease facing a test than one who hasn't. But regardless of the degree of readiness, few students escape butterflies in the stomach. Every person tends to sweat, at least a little.

And there's really little anyone can do to ease the normal tension.

However, there are some general things you can do to help yourself. There are both study tips and test taking tips that can be used to help you take tests efficiently and successfully.

91. What is the first step I should take when approaching a test?

First and foremost, you should avoid cramming for a test. Cramming is naturally equated with tension and anxiety. Furthermore, information hastily stuffed into the mind as quickly drains away. And cramming leaves a student tired and irritable in the morning, hardly prepared for taking a test.

Keep to a study schedule throughout the school year. The schedule should include time for review and test preparation—and time for ample rest the night before an exam.

92. What specific techniques should I use when studying for a test?

When you prepare for a test, concentrate on things you don't know or are unsure of. This may seem obvious and elemental, but many students review material as though they'd never seen it before. Assuming some previous diligence in study, a good deal of material must by now be lodged in the mind. Major attention should be given to content areas you have been having problems with.

A good way to find out what you know and don't know is to review questions from the textbook. Undoubtedly you will miss a few questions—and these are the content areas to concentrate on. Moreover, chapter and unit introductions and summaries should be reviewed automatically. In addition, you should carefully review textbook headings and subheadings, and refer to the questions you developed from those headings as part of application of the SQ3R study method. And organize and carefully review notes you made during lectures and class discussion, or as part of reading sources outside the textbook.

Ask yourself questions that might come up, questions not found in the textbook. By all means study the points the teacher emphasized as the course proceeded. But recognize that you must limit yourself. Time is too short to review *everything* covered in class.

Furthermore, reflect on the teacher's test-giving habits and inclinations. Some teachers, for example, generally prefer objective tests, particularly the kind that call for the recall of specific facts. Others like essay examinations, in which a student must deal not only with facts, but also with trends, concepts, and so on. Some teachers mix up objective and essay questions. In any event, you should gear your studying to the kind of test you are likely to face.

Try to remember the need for physical fitness when going into an exam, part of which means sufficient rest the night before. Some people in addition recommend that a person eat a light breakfast—or lunch—on a test day, and take along a candy bar for additional energy during the test. The brain doesn't seem to operate as well when the stomach is full.

You should also do what you can to build and maintain your confidence in your ability to score well on a test. As we mentioned earlier, even the best of students get a little apprehensive before an exam, so in any case do what you can to keep your morale up.

93. What about students studying together?

In some cases, this can be helpful. If the students are able to "stick to studying," much can be done by way of review, mutual testing, and clarification of ideas through discussion. However, such study sessions can become social situations. And in this case, the result will be a waste of precious time. You are the only one who can decide if joint study sessions will be worthwhile.

94. What is an objective test?

This is a test requiring a single response—selecting the word or phrase that best answers a question or completes a sentence, deciding whether a statement is true or false, filling in a blank with a word or phrase, or matching similar or dissimilar words and phrases.

Objective tests appeal mainly because they can be quickly marked. So a teacher may spend less time on the correction of such a test. Test results can be made available to students relatively quickly.

Ideally speaking, all possibilities from which a student might choose should be sensible and related to the question. Nonsense or unrelated choices should not appear. Each item should be self-contained—that is, two or more items should not say essentially the same thing. Furthermore, the choices should be open to only one interpretation. A good multiple choice test maker tries to avoid the use of such words as "always," "never," "no," "every," "all," and "entirely." In some cases, these words tip a student off; in others, they nullify a question. There should be no "trick" questions.

Here is an example of a multiple choice question, part of a test given after a social studies class had studied revolution:

The phrase "liberty, equality, fraternity" is usually

associated with the

a. American Revolution
b. Russian Revolution
c. French Revolution
d. Chinese Revolution
e. Mexican Revolution

Now a student recalling the Declaration of Independence would realize that the words "equality" and "liberty" figured in the document. "Fraternity" too? The Russian and the Chinese revolutions were Communist, so the idea of equality—and possibly liberty from oppression too—might have been part of them. And maybe fraternity—brotherhood of the proletariat, at least—also. Did the phrase or ideas have anything to do with the Mexican Revolution? Land reform was part of it, so perhaps equality to some extent figured in. The student might arrive at the best response, "c.", through a process of elimination or through simple recall. In any event the question was fair, unambiguous, and demanded some knowledge of course content.

Suppose the question had read: "The phrase 'liberty, equality, fraternity' is *always* associated with the." This would have left the student confused and nullified the question, for the phrase is not *always* associated with the French Revolution.

Suppose, on the other hand, the test maker had left out the Mexican Revolution and had instead made choice "e." "the Yale Wiffenpoof song?" This helps the student, for the phrase has nothing to do with revolutions, and he or she can quickly eliminate the response from consideration. But it represents an example of sloppy test-making.

95. What about other kinds of objective tests?

These include true and false, fill in the blanks, and matching. In many cases success with these kinds of tests rests on good recall, but they also can require a rather broad knowledge of course content. Like multiple choice questions and items, these tests must be read carefully and you should deliberate before responding. And test items here can be both good and poor. For example:

T F Dinosaurs and humans occupied the same territory.

Does this mean at the same time? In that case it's false. Or does it mean the same territory at different times, which would make it true? The question is ambiguous and cannot be answered.

Here's another:

T F Henry Ford made use of the assembly line, which he invented.

It's true that Ford utilized the assembly line. It's false that he invented it. So the question is an unfair one.

Fill in the blank questions can be troublesome too. For example:

The person who developed the theory of evolution was _____.

Charles Darwin   Alfred Wallace
Lamarck   Linnaeus

The impulse would be to select Darwin. But actually all four men had something to do with the concept, and Darwin's and Wallace's views were quite close. They were contemporaries and Wallace, in effect, stepped aside. A better phrasing would be: "The person whose name is most frequently associated with the theory of evolution is _____."

Matching tests can demand something more than simple recall too. Some teachers will include more items in one column than another, for one reason to cut down on student guessing, for another to make the testing sharper. For example:

1. Alexander Hamilton	A. Virginia planter
2. George Washington	B. Revolutionary War officer
3. Thomas Jefferson	C. killed by Aaron Burr in a duel
4. Henry Knox	D. first secretary of the treasury
	E. third President of the U.S.

To be successful here, a person must know that both Washington and Jefferson were Virginia planters, and that Jefferson was the third President. The student must also know that Henry Knox and Washington were Revolutionary War officers. Further, he or she must know that Burr killed Hamilton in a duel, and that Hamilton was the first secretary of the treasury. How would you match these items up?

96. What are some points about taking objective tests that I should keep in mind?

First of all, you should read the directions carefully, twice, in fact, to be sure you understand them. Then you should skim the test to get an idea of its length and how to budget your time.

Budgeting time is extremely important. There might be fifty multiple choice questions to answer in an hour, or perhaps a mixture of objective questions totaling fifty. Perhaps all the questions are true or false and can be dealt with more quickly than an equal number of multiple choice items. A few moments spent at the beginning, planning a time schedule for taking a test, is time well spent. Such planning can help you to avoid panic as the testing period comes to a close.

With respect to objective tests generally, you should read each question carefully. Reword questions if necessary to make them understandable.

First impulses can be correct; the answer that immediately comes to mind is often the right one. But if an answer doesn't come quickly, you should not linger. Note the problem question and move on. In other words, take care of the easy questions first and return later to the others.

Should you guess at an answer? Many standardized tests have a built-in extra penalty for wrong answers, which discourages guessing. But if this is not the case, if only right answers are counted, then you should go ahead and guess. The chances of being right vary with the number of choices. If it's a true or false item, the chances are fifty-fifty—not bad odds.

When planning your time, you should allow some at the end to check over the test. This is simply to make sure that you have responded to all of the items, and to catch any inadvertent "boners."

97. What are essay exams?

Ordinarily, essay exams require a student to pull together various pieces of information, as well as an understanding of concepts, and answer a question in clear, readable prose. Essay questions are usually easy to formulate, but they do require time to read and correct. And subjective elements can enter into the correction of essay exams.

For example, many teachers react negatively, at least

unconsciously, to poor penmanship. Almost everyone does. So a person with poor penmanship is automatically penalized whether a teacher intends to do so or not. More properly speaking, a student who cannot write legibly penalizes him or herself. So you should try to develop at least a legible hand. It makes a difference in essay tests.

At the same time, a teacher might not be sure just how many points a student should make in an essay question to merit an "A" or a "B" and so on. Some teachers even vary their expectations for individual students. A wise teacher, after he or she forms an essay question, will answer it, and then list the points students should make. This provides an objective standard against which to judge each student's paper.

98. What are some examples of essay questions?

Such questions vary greatly and some are broader than others. Some essay questions demand an ability to recall many facts and details. Others concentrate more on a need to demonstrate an understanding of concepts or broad issues.

One example of an essay question might be: "Argue pro or con: the French Revolution was inevitable." Another might be: "Describe the process of photosynthesis." Another: "Explain Newton's three laws of motion." And yet another: "Describe and analyze the motivations behind the writing of the Constitution of the United States."

99. Are there any points to watch on essay tests?

Here again you should read questions carefully, usually twice at least. You should be clear about the meaning of such words as "evaluate," "analyze," "explain," and "contrast."

And organizing time is as important when taking an essay test as with any other test. Before beginning to write, you should also organize your thoughts. It's wise for you to make a brief outline or at least to jot down the points you intend to cover. Time spent on such preparation pays off. Having the test questions firmly in mind, as well as the way you intend to organize your response to those questions, greatly increases the likelihood of a successful result.

You should be sure to write legibly, even if this means slowing down. It's better to leave out a point or two than to hand in a paper on which most or all of the points—regardless of how made—suffer from poor penmanship.

Finally, as with objective tests, you should allow time near the end of the testing period to reread what you have written. At this time, you should correct errors in spelling, punctuation, and so on, and perhaps insert some information to make an answer clearer.

100. Is there anything in particular to watch for when taking tests that a computer will score?

Yes, one thing especially. Ordinarily you will have to make a mark corresponding to the choice you have made. In the process of scoring the test an electronic device will pick up and record marks inserted in the proper place. In many cases a student is required to find a number on a separate sheet matching the test item number, then follow across along a grid to place the mark. If the student is in a hurry, and students often are, it is very easy to inadvertently mark the wrong column. So you must be doubly careful when taking such a test

101, Can tests help me to improve my performance in school?

Yes, because tests give you the opportunity to find out in which areas you need additional work. You should keep the tests you have taken. Study the results, pinpointing both items on which you did well and items on which you did poorly.

Discuss test results with your teacher. But avoid turning such a discussion into an argument over the grade. Instead, ask for clarification of items which you got wrong. Find out what you can do to increase your understanding of difficult content areas.

Finally, this is a key item. Avoid considering your test results from the point-of-view of the grade received. Instead, use test results as one gauge of achievement and as the basis upon which to plan for further study.

Index

The editors of "101 Easy Ways to Get Better Grades" hope that you will use this Index creatively and intelligently, as a study tool in itself. The Index, like those in your textbooks, is here to help you find vital information. This is a typical entry:

Outline, 62–63

Note that the numbers refer to page numbers (not the question numbers) in the text.

Some headings in the Index contain additional information. "See" or "see also" listings direct you to other headings in the Index that may have the information you are seeking. An example of such a listing is as follows: "Words, see Vocabulary."

World Book Encyclopedia, Inc. offers a wide range of educational and reference materials, including a video—"How to Study." This 45-minute VHS tape combines the appeal of television with an easy-to-use formula for developing successful study habits. For more information on World Book's "How to Study" video, as well as our wide selection of educational and reference books, please write:
World Book Encyclopedia, Inc.
P.O. Box 3405, Chicago, Illinois 60654-9980.

Notes

Notes

Notes

Notes

Notes

Notes